CONTEXTS IN LITERATURE

Romanticism

David Stevens

Series Editor: Adrian Barlow

CAMBRIDGE
UNIVERSITY

CAMBRIDGE UNIVERSITY PRESS
Cambridge, New York, Melbourne, Madrid, Cape Town,
Singapore, São Paulo, Delhi, Tokyo, Mexico City

Cambridge University Press
The Edinburgh Building, Cambridge CB2 8RU, UK

www.cambridge.org
Information on this title: www.cambridge.org/9780521753722

First published 2004
6th printing 2011

Printed in the United Kingdom at the University Press, Cambridge

A catalogue record for this publication is available from the British Library

ACKNOWLEDGEMENTS
The author and publishers wish to thank the following for permission to use
copyright material:

Curtis Brown Ltd, London, on behalf of Eric Robinson for John Clare, 'I Am', edited
by Eric Robinson. Copyright © Eric Robinson 1984; Oxford University Press for
extracts from Dorothy Wordsworth, The Grasmere Journals (1801–1802), edited
by M Moorman (1973), entries – 22.11.1801, 24.11.01, 29.11.01, 18.3.02.

Every effort has been made to reach copyright holders; the publishers would like to
hear from anyone whose rights they have unknowingly infringed.

ISBN 978-0-521-75372-2 Paperback

Prepared for publication by Gill Stacey
Designed by Tattersall Hammarling & Silk
Cover illustration: The Wanderer above the Sea of fog, 1818 (oil on canvas)
by Caspar David Friedrich (1774–1840), The Bridgeman Art Library,
London/Hamburg, Kunsthalle, Hamburg, Germany

Contents

Time line

Date	Social / political context	Romanticism
1757		Burke *A Philosophical Enquiry*. William Blake born.
1762		Rousseau *Emile*.
1764		Walpole *The Castle of Otranto*.
1770	Cook lands in Australia.	Chatterton's suicide. William Wordsworth born.
1772		Samuel Taylor Coleridge born.
1774	Louis XVI King of France.	
1775	American War of Independence begins. James Watts invents steam engine.	J.M. Turner (artist) born. Jane Austen born.
1776	American Declaration of Independence.	John Constable (artist) born.
1780	Anti-Catholic Gordon riots.	
1781	Defeat of Britain in American War of Independence.	Immanuel Kant *Critique of Pure Reason* (philosophy).
1782	Peace of Versailles between Britain, France and America.	Blake *Poetical Sketches*.
1786		Beckford *Vathek*.
1787	American Constitution signed.	
1788		George Gordon Byron born.
1789	French Revolution starts. George Washington first US President.	Blake *Songs of Innocence*.
1790		Burke *Reflections on the Revolution in France*.
1791		Paine *The Rights of Man (Part 1)*.
1792	France declared a Republic. Terror begins (to 1794).	Wollstonecraft *A Vindication of the Rights of Woman*. Percy Bysshe Shelley born.
1793	Execution of Louis XVI and Marie Antoinette. France and Britain at war.	David's painting 'The Death of Marat'. Blake *The Marriage of Heaven and Hell*. John Clare born.
1794	Robespierre murdered.	Blake *Songs of Experience*. Godwin *Caleb Williams*. Ann Radcliffe *Mysteries of Udolpho*.
1795		John Keats born.
1796		Lewis *The Monk*.
1798	Continuing European wars.	Friedrich Schlegel *Athenaeum*. Wordsworth and Coleridge *Lyrical Ballads*.
1799	Napoleon 1st Consul of France. Combination Acts in Britain prohibit Trade Unions.	
1802	Peace of Amiens (to 1803) between Britain and France.	
1804	Napoleon Emperor of France.	Blake begins *Jerusalem* (prophetic book).
1805	Battle of Trafalgar: British naval victory over France and Spain.	Wordsworth *The Prelude*.

Date	Social / political context	Romanticism
1810		Scott 'The Lady of the Lake'.
1811	Luddite unrest in Britain. Prince of Wales becomes Regent, as George III increasingly insane.	Austen *Sense and Sensibility*.
1812	French retreat from Moscow.	
1813		Shelley 'Queen Mab'. Austen *Pride and Prejudice*. Southey made poet laureate.
1814	George Stephenson constructs a working steam locomotive.	
1815	Napoleon finally defeated at Waterloo: end of French war. Economic depression in Britain.	
1816		Coleridge 'Kubla Khan', 'Christabel'. Cobbett founds *Political Register*, a political journal.
1817		Keats *Poems*. Coleridge *Biographia Literaria*. Death of Jane Austen.
1818		Mary Shelley *Frankenstein*. Keats 'Endymion'. Coleridge lectures on philosophy.
1819	Peterloo massacre: militia attack peaceful demonstration.	Byron 'Don Juan' I and II (the rest published 1819–1824)
1820	Death of George III; Prince Regent becomes George IV.	Clare *Poems Descriptive of Rural Life*. Shelley 'Prometheus Unbound'. Blake completes *Jerusalem*.
1821	Greek War of Independence, lasting until 1828.	Constable 'The Hay Wain'. Death of Keats. De Quincey *Confessions of an English Opium Eater*.
1822		Death of Shelley.
1824		Death of Byron at Missolonghi, Greece.
1825	Stockton – Darlington railway.	Beethoven's 9th Symphony performed in London.
1827		Death of Blake. Death of Beethoven. Clare *The Shepherd's Calender*.
1829	Catholic emancipation in Britain.	
1831	Charles Darwin's Pacific voyages in the *Beagle*.	
1832	Reform Act: broader franchise.	
1833	British Factory Act prohibiting employment of children under 9.	
1834	Tolpuddle Martyrs transported. Poor Law Amendment Act: establishment of workhouses. Slavery abolished in British Empire.	Death of Coleridge. Death of Charles Lamb.

Introduction

To describe someone or something as 'romantic' can suggest a huge, perhaps confusing, range of possibilities. The term may be applied, for example, to the traditional Mills and Boon novel, with its characteristically subservient young women and darkly brooding men. It may be applied to the sorts of rhyming couplets found in Valentine cards to accompany the similarly romantic gesture of giving extravagant bouquets of flowers. It may also refer to any affectionate relationship, as in the term 'romantically linked'. Alternatively, of course, it might denote a particular type of artistic expression in the context of literature, the visual arts, dance, drama or music. These are just a few of the many possible uses of the term. This book will focus primarily on the last of these examples – a mode of artistic expression – and especially on the literary. But at the same time other possibilities, even those alluded to above, are not called 'romantic' by accident. There may well be connections worth exploring.

Part of the function of this book is to offer some guidance through the diversity of uses and meanings of the word 'romantic', not in terms of fixed definitions or essential qualifying characteristics, but rather in giving a practically helpful framework for questions and explorations. The focus throughout tends to be on the Western European cultural world of the latter half of the 18th century and the first half of the 19th, as befits English literary study, but the context is far broader. It will include, for example, the suggestion that whatever is romantic in the arts continues as a possible mode of expression to this day, and was by no means limited to the period intensively studied – however much validity there may be in describing that period as Romantic. Please note here the use of upper case initial letter, suggesting a particular cultural entity, not simply a loosely applied adjective. There may be a certain tension here between the twin approaches: the one inclusive and eclectic, covering all sorts of human activities and attitudes; the other – Romanticism as an upper case 'ism' – seeking sharp focus and clarity of contextual definition.

Critics and commentators have presented, and still do, a vast range of sometimes conflicting opinions on the nature of the Romantic. This can be bewildering, especially in the context of present-day diversification of critical opinion and increasing specialisation of study. There are tensions and oppositions here too, but also the possibilities of creative cross-fertilisation. Another of the main aims of this book is to help the reader achieve some degree of critical synthesis – combining aspects of various views to create a coherent appraisal – through seeing Romantic texts in context. Consider, for example, these views of the Romantic:

What we see when we look at the period as a whole is rather an extraordinary flowering and richness of creativity, involving individual writers who were drawn to think and write in new ways, and who sometimes enjoyed collaborative relationships with other individuals. It is only in retrospect that each can be seen as a larger pattern of 'Romantic' thinking and writing.

(from John Beer 'Literature' in *The Romantic Age in Britain*, ed. Boris Ford, 1992)

The opposition between Classicism and Romanticism is persistent and misleading, for the Romantic imagination was assimilative: exploring the past, the Romantics recovered more than they rejected, expanding their heritage through a revival of native themes and subjects that had been dismissed as too vulgar, common, or undignified for the tastes of Augustan gentlemen.

(from Marilyn Gaull *English Romanticism: The Human Context*, 1988)

Politically it [Romanticism] was inspired by the revolutions in America and France ... Emotionally it expressed an extreme assertion of the self and the value of individual experience ... together with the sense of the infinite and the transcendental. Socially it championed progressive causes ... The stylistic keynote of Romanticism is intensity, and its watchword is 'Imagination'.

(from *The Oxford Companion to English Literature*, ed. Margaret Drabble, 1985)

The three writers quoted above form just a small sample of the many commentators and critics whose views will be encountered in this book. Some of the points they raise, even at this early stage, may only be understood in the contexts of the period they are writing about and of their various schools of critical thought. There is an underlying purpose here: to see Romanticism (in particular Romantic literature) in context – or rather in a series of contexts, including diverse and often challenging critical contexts. Indeed, in order to understand Romanticism and any of its artistic manifestations, it is vital to engage fully across a range of connected areas: with contemporary historical and cultural contexts; with the variety of art forms; with critical opinion; with the concerns of the modern age; and with the particular interests and obsessions of the texts themselves. The extracts and whole short texts included in this book are intended to give a flavour of Romantic writing across a fairly broad range of authors, genres and periods. This must remain, however, a tasting session which may be followed up by a more comprehensive exploration of some of the key texts, including those listed at the end of the book. There is, as ever, a balance to be achieved between critical distance and personal engagement, but it is worth bearing in mind that, above all else, it is engagement which characterises the Romantic approach to life and the arts. This, then, is the underlying message of the book.

How the book is organised

Part 1: Approaching Romanticism
Part 1 is a survey of Romanticism, particularly as seen through its literature. It examines the historical and cultural trends which provided the contexts for the development of Romanticism in the 18th and 19th centuries.

Part 2: Approaching the texts
Part 2 considers the different elements that make a text essentially 'Romantic', and relates these to a range of Romantic literature.

Part 3: Texts and extracts
Part 3 contains texts and extracts to illustrate key themes and points from the rest of the book, or to suggest a focus for tasks and assignments.

Part 4: Critical approaches
Part 4 explores the different ways in which critics and readers have responded to Romantic literature.

Part 5: How to write about Romanticism
Part 5 offers guidelines and assignments for students covering the topic as part of an advanced course in literary studies.

Part 6: Resources
Part 6 contains guidance for further reading and exploration, a glossary and index. (Terms which appear in the glossary are highlighted in bold type when they first appear in the main text.)

At different points in the book there are tasks and assignments suggesting a range of contexts through which students might approach an understanding of Romanticism and of particular works.

1 | Approaching Romanticism

- What are the significant social, political and cultural events and developments of the period from approximately 1750 to 1850?

- What historical information and insights may be helpful in coming to and developing a thorough understanding of literature, particularly Romantic texts, written during this period?

- What possible meanings are there for the term 'Romantic' in the historical context?

- What is the place of the Romantic, in any of its possible senses, in the modern world?

Tensions and possible definitions

The terms 'Romanticism' or 'Romantic' are used frequently in discussion or writing about the arts and their cultural context over the past 200 years – an assertion that can easily be verified through even a cursory glance at relevant books or web-sites. However this widespread use of the term can be misleading, and beguiling in its apparent simplicity. For behind the commonly understood notion of what Romanticism actually is – what it stands for in artistic terms – lie a number of tensions, controversies, confusions and contradictions. As with so much else, especially when dealing with literary criticism in cultural contexts, the deeper one goes the less certain any meaning seems. It may well be that an important part of whatever Romanticism turns out to be is the suggestion that we should be able to live with, and even creatively celebrate, this uncertainty. Nevertheless, there is also a need to find some sort of common ground and clarity in understanding Romanticism, without which it would become to all intents and purposes meaningless. It is the underlying purpose of this book to try to establish this common ground, whilst simultaneously acknowledging diversity of meaning, interpretation and creative manifestation.

Margaret Drabble's definition of Romanticism has already been quoted in the Introduction; the emphasis is on emotion, imagination, individuality and a certain sense of opposition to what had gone before – namely, the **Enlightenment** of the late 17th and 18th centuries with its espousal of reason as the key to all understanding. Another opening quotation, from John Beer, stresses creativity; the third, by Marilyn Gaull, gives a sense of reaction against **Classicism**. Already it should be clear that there is some common ground here. One problem, however, is that none of these terms can be pinned down by a simple definition, because they are all subject partly to culturally formed value systems, and partly to the slipperiness of language itself.

Take the word 'imagination': does it imply a positive, creatively liberating force without which nothing could be achieved by human beings; or does it refer to a possibly dangerous escapist position, refusing to confront reality? Perhaps there are elements of both in the semantic field – the range of feasible meanings, connotations and associations – of the word, and the tension between the two opposing views gives rise to interesting creative possibilities at the heart of whatever Romanticism may be. Again, it is the exploration of such areas, rather than their pinning down, that is at the heart of understanding, and the sense of context is the map needed for this exploration.

▶ What associations does the word 'imagination' have in your mind? What would your own definition include?

The birth of Romanticism

The features of the Romantic landscape to be explored are many and varied, changing over time and in appearance depending on the vantage point. The use of the term 'Romantic' is in itself significant, and has been understood differently at different times. In fact, it only gained common currency towards the end of the period studied here, and seems to have emanated from German origins – an interesting pointer to the international, or at least European, scope of the development of Romanticism. In Britain in the second half of the 18th century, there had been references to 'romances', a form somewhere between a long narrative poem or ballad and a folk tale. These romances – frequently French in origin, then translated – often featured chivalrous deeds in past ages. Clearly, there is a semantic link between the terms 'romance' and 'Romanticism', but as has happened so often in the history of words, the term 'romance' was originally used disparagingly. In 1751, for example, in a review of Smollet's *Peregrine Pickle*, John Cleland belittled

> ... romances and novels which turn upon characters out of nature, monsters of perfection, feats of chivalry, fairy enchantments, and the whole train of the marvellously absurd [which] transport the reader unprofitably into the clouds.

A few years later, in 1755, Dr. Johnson (1709–1784) decried the 'Romantick' as 'wild, ... improbable; false, ... fanciful'. Later in the century, however, when the term had become more widely used, the 'romance' was seen more positively – especially in the context of the taste for all things gothic. The **gothic** author Clara

Reeve (1729–1807), for instance, in her appropriately titled *The Progress of Romance* (1785) praised the form as 'an heroic fable, which treats of fabulous persons and things'. The birth of what came to be called Romanticism occurred in the latter part of the 18th century, as popular and critical taste began to endorse the characteristics of the romance, and to transfer some of these characteristics – particularly the fascination with the imaginatively exotic and with extremes of emotion – to other art forms. The result, as the philosopher Isaiah Berlin has noted, was 'a shift of consciousness [that] cracked the backbone of European thought'.

National and international perspectives

So the term 'Romanticism' gradually acquired its meaning, simultaneously accruing new connotations and associations – as do all new words entering the flow of a living language. One important association was the sense of the Romantic in opposition to the order and formal symmetry of what was called the Classical, or Neo-Classical (to suggest a recovery of ancient Greek and Roman cultures), with its strong emphasis on civilised good order. The Classical aesthetic – or way of conceiving and viewing art – had itself derived from Greek and Roman models. As early as 1774 the literary historian Thomas Wharton noted the distinction in his *History of English Poetry* (1774–1781):

> That peculiar and arbitrary species of Fiction which we commonly call Romantic, was entirely unknown to the writers of Greece and Rome.
> … [These fictions] formed the groundwork of that species of fabulous narrative called romance.

Elsewhere, Wharton mentions, in the same context, poets such as Edmund Spenser (1552–1599) and English mythical heroes like King Arthur. The Englishness of all this, as noted in the title of Wharton's book, was no accident: in a sense, it indicated a growing national need to move away from Classical models in favour of something distinctively English – or, increasingly, British. In this there was a vivid reflection of what was happening in Germany, which was then not a single nation but a collection of separate states, and where there was a fast developing nationalist movement. There was also cross-fertilisation of ideas between intellectuals and artists in Britain and Germany, given sharp focus through the influence of radical and revolutionary ideas inspired by the French Revolution in 1789, and through the later wars against Napoleonic France.

A series of lectures given in Berlin between 1801 and 1804 by the German philosopher and critic, August Wilhelm Schlegel (1767–1845), is widely regarded as one of the first self-consciously defining moments for Romanticism. Meanwhile, Schlegel's younger brother Friedrich (1772–1829) was applying ideas about the

Romantic to modern poetry, asserting, for example, that 'Romantic poetry is a progressive universal poetry'. Certainly, there are some powerful insights into the nature of the arts at the beginning of the 19th century, many of which found ready followers and disseminators in Britain. Of these, Samuel Taylor Coleridge (1772–1834) was the most influential (although he was not always too fastidious about naming his sources). The significance of August Schlegel's lectures makes them worth quoting in some detail:

> The whole play of vital motion hinges on harmony and contrast. Why should this phenomenon not also recur on a grander scale in the history of mankind? Perhaps in this notion the true key could be found to the ancient and modern history of poetry and the fine arts. Those who have accepted this have invented for the particular spirit of modern art, in contrast to ancient and classical, the name 'romantic'. The term is certainly not inappropriate. The word is derived from romance …
>
> … the poetry of the ancients was the poetry of possession, ours is that of longing; the former is firmly rooted in the soil of the present, the latter hovers between recollection and yearning. … Among the moderns feeling has become altogether more intense, imagination more ethereal, thought more contemplative.

There are many insights and claims here, and the themes will be revisited throughout this book. Worth noting, especially, is the sense of newness – 'the moderns' – and the liberating quality this newness inspires. This has implications for the study of Romanticism generally: Romantic texts cannot go on being 'new' indefinitely. However, the *study* of Romantic artefacts may be constantly renewed, and as a result interpretations will be modified, and creative engagement may be perpetually refreshed. This indeed is the spirit of Romanticism: if it means anything, it must constantly re-invent, rediscover and re-assert itself. Another German commentator, and a contemporary of the Schlegel brothers, Friedrich Hardenberg (1772–1801; known as 'Novalis') emphasised this quality: 'The world must be romanticised. So its original meaning will again be found. To romanticise is nothing other than an exponential heightening.'

The evidence just quoted may suggest that contemporaries were aware of something Romantic in the air. However, it would be a mistake to think of Romanticism as anything like a coherent movement or philosophy. With hindsight, of course, it is possible to select historical evidence to justify a particular point of view, but this can be misleading. As Marilyn Butler, a modern critic and historian of Romanticism, maintains, 'Romanticism, in the full rich sense in which we now know it, is a posthumous movement; something different was experienced at the time.' (from *Romantics, Rebels and Reactionaries*, 1981). In other words, developing the landscape metaphor touched on above, those people closely involved at the time of the Romantic revolution were generally caught up in their own localities and paths and didn't notice any larger topographical change, anything bigger. Perhaps it is only when the passage of time allows some distance that the contours of a new landscape, mapped in more detail, become discernible. Nor does the uncertainty end here. Another modern commentator, Hugh Honour, suggests:

> The word Romanticism has come to be used in a bewildering variety of ways, as a term of abuse or praise, as a chronological, aesthetic or psychological category, to describe erotic emotions or purely cerebral processes. As none of these forms of usage is indefensible, and all may be traced back to the early Nineteenth Century, those who have attempted to establish a precise definition have often given up in despair.
>
> (from *Romanticism*, 1991)

The point here, however, lies in knowing what to look for: precision is likely to be elusive, but the very diversity of Romanticism does offer potentially liberating possibilities in its exploration. In the end, moreover, Romanticism does seem to embody certain key characteristics; and as a historical phenomenon, as William Vaughan puts it, '… whatever else is said about the Romantic movement, no one can deny that it really did happen' (from *Romantic Art*, 1994). So, what are these key characteristics?

▶ Look carefully at what Marilyn Butler and Hugh Honour have to say about Romanticism. Do they support or contradict each other?

Key characteristics of Romanticism

The list below is intended as a guiding summary. The various themes and characteristics it comprises make sense only within the context of further exploratory study – partly using this book, but also ranging further and wider beyond its boundaries. Neither is the list limited only to Romantic literature, but is intended to apply loosely to all art forms. There is, further, a great deal of overlap, in that some points refer strongly to certain individuals within the broad area of Romanticism and not to others. For the purposes of this list the past tense has been used, suggesting the historical period most closely associated with Romanticism. However, many of the attitudes and ideas here could easily be held by people today, who have been either consciously or unconsciously influenced by Romanticism.

- Hitherto unknown levels of importance and prestige tended to attach to individuals and their particular creative talents. Frequently, this was in an iconoclastic sense: in other words, departing from, and sometimes seeking to dismantle altogether, the traditional conventions in the appropriate genre, or type of writing.

- Following from this point, subjectivity (a strongly personal viewpoint, often in a visionary sense) was valued highly; sometimes this was at the expense of the quest for scientific, rationally ascertained objectivity (or what is demonstrably true in the 'real' world).

- The form and meaning of this subjective experience often aspired to a spiritual, sometimes mystical, significance, expressed also in quasi-religious symbolic language. As such, there was a real, or perceived, threat to established religion and its values.

- At a time when nature was just beginning to be threatened by the gathering forces of urbanisation and industrialisation, it acquired greater value – especially in its grander, wilder aspects. For some, veneration of nature was akin to a religious experience.

- Conventional and time-honoured codes of morality were increasingly questioned, especially by the more radical Romantics, in favour of more individualistic, and personally liberating, ethical codes.

- By extension, the existing social order was often found wanting in its embodiment of traditional value systems. Romantics could be fiercely individualistic on the one hand, and radically socialist on the other. Not infrequently, there was the possibility of contradiction, or at least tension, here.

- Politically, Romantics were generally in favour of radical, or even revolutionary, change – at least in the early days of Romanticism. Subsequently, a split is discernible between those who retained this position, and others who became more conservative and individualistic, and who developed notions of society as developing in organic rather than revolutionary ways.

- Rationality – the belief that an outlook and procedures based on the application of reason are the most apt for humanity – was found wanting. Emotions, sometimes in extreme, passionate form, were valued highly by Romantics.

- Romantics frequently focused on and admired the state of innocence, and the accompanying senses of wonder, alienation, or even terror and madness.

- As implied by the previous point, there was often great fascination for altered states of consciousness, sometimes drug-induced, and for art forms which both helped to achieve and vividly express such states; for example, Coleridge's mythical location 'Xanadu' from his poem 'Kubla Khan'.

- Hero-figures and heroic deeds were accorded huge significance, expressed dramatically throughout different art forms, and often through chosen lifestyles. Lord Byron is perhaps the most notable example here.

- An appropriate national past was discovered – or sometimes fabricated – in an attempt to discern and continue a tradition of exoticism and heroism. There was a fascination for myths and legends from the distant past, as recounted in ballads and folk tales.

- Simultaneously, and sometimes confusingly, rebellious anti-heroes were also sought out, invented or re-interpreted, for example, Prometheus for Mary Shelley, and Milton's Satan for William Blake.

All of these points will be explored more fully in a variety of contexts throughout this book. Taken together, they suggest, as the American critic Arthur Lovejoy wrote in 1924, that

> ... we should learn to use the word 'Romanticism' in the plural. ... What is needed is that any study of the subject should begin with a recognition of a *prima facie* plurality of Romanticisms, of possibly quite distinct thought-complexes, a number of which may appear in one country.

The French poet Charles Baudelaire (1821–1867), a Romantic himself, made the vital point that 'Romanticism is precisely situated neither in choice of subject, nor in exact truth, but in a way of feeling'. In order to understand this way of feeling more profoundly, it is necessary to examine in some detail the contextual factors at work. As a guiding principle, Marilyn Butler's insight rings true: 'No form is confined to a single political message. Everything turns on how it is used, and on how the public at a given time is ready to read it.' (from *Romantics, Rebels and Reactionaries*, 1981). And the reading must be in the fullest, suggestive sense of the word: not only in the reading of printed text, but also in the ways we might 'read' a situation, for example, or 'read' someone's character.

▶ Examine again the various key characteristics of Romanticism listed above, and try relating them to modern culture and the arts. Aim to come to some sort of judgement as to whether the examples chosen from modern culture meet any, some or all of the tentative criteria for Romanticism.

    You may wish to look at examples from:

- music across a range of styles and genres
- films and television drama

- literature in various forms intended for various readerships
- advertising imagery and the arts of persuasion
- developments in modern art.

As a result of your research, to what extent would you say the modern age – particularly in its cultural manifestations in the broadest sense – is essentially Romantic?

The historical and political contexts of Romanticism

Placing the exponents of Romanticism in historical and political context is not simply a matter of 'framing' them in a particular time and place, but rather of exploring their active involvement in the events and movements of the day. In a time of profound and widespread social and political upheaval, from which we are still feeling the reverberations today, the influence of the Romantics was often considerable. Their involvement could take many forms, but perhaps the nearest we can get to a common factor is the sense of creative expression shared by so many Romantics across a wide range of genres and styles. The arts and politics became inextricably linked, and this is one of the most lasting legacies of Romanticism.

It would be difficult to over-estimate the impact of the key historical trends occurring during the period of Romanticism: there were political and social revolutions the like and speed of which had never previously been experienced. Overshadowing all other events was the cataclysmic influence of the French Revolution of 1789, which ' … sharpened the historical sense in a way that no other event had ever done' (Hugh Honour in *Romanticism*, 1991).

(As a way of attempting to map these historical changes against some of the most significant events of Romanticism, the Time line on pages 6–7 may help to give a fuller perspective.)

In the field of politics (defined broadly as opposed to any narrow conception of party or parliamentary politics), the Romantics were intensely active in both thought and deed. This in itself was something of a departure: the link between creative endeavour and politics had never before been so explicit, had never been such a liberating, energising force. The focus changed too, and reflected a shift in emphasis, away from the concerns of royalty and the aristocracy as somehow embodying the affairs of state, towards far more democratic notions of politics. In this the Romantics were self-consciously breaking new ground. By 1821 the Romantic poet, Percy Bysshe Shelley (1792–1822), was able to claim in his *A Defence of Poetry* that poets revealed 'less their spirit than the spirit of the age', and, potentially at least, 'are the unacknowledged legislators of the world'.

As Marilyn Gaull writes:

> When Homer sang of national wars, or Chaucer performed at court, or Shakespeare dramatised the chronicles of kings, politics and poetry shared the same frame of reference: the activities and interests of the aristocracy, the centre of political power. But during the Romantic period, poets became active in political activities that had no poetic precedence, for they lived in an age of democratic revolution, engaged in political dissent, and identified with the people.
>
> (from *English Romanticism: The Human Context*, 1988)

Ideas and philosophies

One of the key issues central to any historical study, and pertinent to the exploration of Romanticism, is the question of how far new ideas and philosophies influence, or even determine, the course of history. Certain elements of Romanticism might suggest that the influence is considerable, perhaps crucial: the emphasis on hero figures and heroic deeds, for example, or the general sense of the importance of new ways of looking at the world. In its extreme form, this view (that ideas determine history) has been termed philosophical idealism, and philosophers broadly influential in the development of Romanticism, such as Kant, Hegel or even Coleridge, were central figures here. This may be beguiling, of course, in that the Romantics themselves need not necessarily be the most trustworthy commentators on the movement – if it can be called this – of which they were part.

An alternative, opposing, view of history suggests that ideas – and the people who think them – are essentially the product of actual historical forces of a social, political and economic nature. Karl Marx, the founder of Communism, whose own ideas developed towards the end of the Romantic period (his 'Communist Manifesto' was published amidst the revolutionary ferment of 1848) did much to promote such a view of history. In its extreme form, this interpretation of history has been termed historical materialism. Many modern Marxists, however, are at pains to deny that Marx was ever a crude historical materialist. They point instead to his development of Hegel's notion of the dialectical processes of historical change – the suggestion that ideas and events are inextricably linked and that the attempt to separate them to see which comes first is ultimately futile. Further, that the conflict between historical forces – which may include philosophies and artistic creations – creates new realities, born of struggle: essentially, a synthesis. This may well be a helpful tool in understanding Romanticism, itself clearly born of intense struggles in the realms of philosophies and historical events.

The influence of the Enlightenment

The culture of the 18th century, and the essential context of the birth of Romanticism, was that of the Enlightenment. As with so much else, the meaning of this term is fraught with difficulties and tensions; nevertheless, it was the dominant cultural force of the time – and for its adherents, it was a profoundly civilising influence. Key figures here, stretching back to the intellectual achievements of the 17th century, were the rationalist philosophers Descartes, Bacon and Locke, and scientists such as Isaac Newton. The central tenet of the Enlightenment was that through a spirit of rational, scientific enquiry humanity could realistically aspire to an ideal of peace and harmony. For some, even ultimate perfection was possible. The obstacles to this perfection were seen to be those inherited from a discredited past: prejudice, irrational beliefs, emotional instability and extravagance of feeling. In asserting this, Enlightenment thinkers often sought inspiration from a different, and more distant past: the period of history known as the Classical, based on first the Greek and later the Roman empires and cultures. In terms of artistic expression, the Enlightenment way of thinking emphasised structural order, harmony, symmetrical proportion, and carefully maintained boundaries in what was acceptable: in other words, or so it was felt, the fundamentals of good taste. Such a position, because of the professed inspiration from classical models, became known as the Neo-Classical.

Romanticism can be seen as a reaction against all the Enlightenment stood for, and for much of the 19th and 20th centuries this was the dominant interpretation. A more subtle sense of how Romanticism arose from its 18th century context tends to see both continuities and contrasts, as opposed to a sharply dividing watershed between an ordered Neo-Classical outlook on the one hand and a rebellious, inspired Romanticism on the other. Several characteristics which are generally seen as quintessentially Romantic were already gaining influence and credibility in the first half of the 18th century, including political idealism, attraction to nature, a fondness for children and the child-like, and a questioning of orthodox religious positions. Radical political philosophers such as Thomas Paine (1737–1809) and William Godwin (1756–1836), influential in both the American and French Revolutions as well as in British radicalism, had their roots firmly in Enlightenment ideas on the perfectibility of humanity and in belief in reason as the essential means of attaining it. William Blake, regarded as one of the most profoundly Romantic of British poets and artists – for he is famous as both – shared many Enlightenment attitudes: his insistence on the need for firm outline of form in art and the disarming simplicity of his early 'Poetical Sketches', for example.

Nevertheless, it would be a mistake to ascribe too much significance to continuities like these, for there were clear discontinuities too – perhaps more significant in the general trend of cultural and social history. As the 18th century wore on, many intellectuals and artists realised that Enlightenment ways of thinking, progressive and useful though they had been, had severe limitations. Chief amongst these misgivings was the suspicion that vast areas of human experience – the emotional, the mystical, the irrational, the imaginative – were in danger of being ignored. And not only that: as Blake, in particular, saw, if such powerful elements of what it is to be human are ignored or suppressed, they are likely to assert themselves all the more destructively. The Spanish artist Goya (1746–1848) thought much the same: in one of his most telling pictures, destructive, threatening creatures encircle a sleeping man, his head slumped on a desk which bears the inscription (in Spanish) 'The sleep of reason produces monsters.' Goya's explanatory notes amplify the assertion: 'Fantasy abandoned by reason produces impossible monsters; united with it she is the mother of the arts and origin of its marvels.' Tellingly, Romantics like Blake and Goya, in their different ways, were beginning to say similar things, stressing not the abandonment of reason, but its fruitful partnership with and recognition of emotion and imagination. As Blake put it in *The Marriage of Heaven and Hell*, 'Energy is the only life, and is from the body; and reason is the bound or outward circumference of energy.' It may well be, of course, that it was precisely because the beneficiaries of scientific and rational progress during the Enlightenment felt safe in their relative material comfort and security that they were now able to dabble in areas of experience beyond the normal boundaries. Whatever the cause, there certainly was something of a 'sea change', as summarised by the art historian David Blayney Brown:

> Like a great tide on the turn, the focus of philosophical enquiry began to change from the objective to the subjective, and a new generation began to explore the potential of emotion and instinct rather than the conscious mind, of integrity rather than obedience, of sufferings, sorrows and fear as well as joy, of the humble and natural instead of sophistication, of the idiosyncratic instead of the ideal. ... Not since the Renaissance had such a profound change come over Western consciousness. ... Romanticism emphasised individual experience, feeling and expression.
>
> (from *Romanticism*, 2001)

These are large claims; in order to verify or challenge them, it is necessary to study further some of the artistic expressions of early Romanticism.

▶ Consider some of the artistic expressions of early Romanticism, if possible comparing them to examples of what had gone before in more classical form. You may like to study some of the following to get a fuller sense of the context of Romanticism:

- The painting 'The Nightmare' (1782) by Henry Fuseli (1741–1825)
- The text and accompanying illustrations in *The Marriage of Heaven and Hell* (1793) by William Blake
- The painting 'Chatterton receiving Poison from the Spirit of Despair' (1780) by John Flaxman (1755–1826)
- Symphony no 3, *The Eroica* (1804) by Ludwig van Beethoven (1770–1827)
- The painting 'Snow Storm: Hannibal and his Army crossing the Alps' (1812) by William Turner (1775–1851)
- The painting 'The Cross in the Mountains' (1808) by Caspar David Friedrich (1774–1840)

The impact of revolution, war and political radicalism

The impact of the French Revolution of 1789 on European culture and politics was felt as strongly and consciously at the time as it has been judged by historians since. This revolution, which led directly to the execution of Louis XVI, the Terror, the rise of Napoleon, political divisions throughout Europe, and over 20 years of war in Europe and beyond, was seen by many as sharply dividing the past from a new type of future. For some this was a terrifying prospect, for others it was greeted optimistically; and for many in the latter group – often Romantics – this optimism turned to disappointment and disillusion. It has been suggested, sometimes by the Romantics themselves, that the ferment created by the Romantic notion of rebellious energy giving life its power was responsible for the French Revolution. While it may not be helpful to try to disentangle ideas from events, philosophies from actualities, what is certain is that Romantic attitudes closely accompanied revolution, radicalism and, subsequently, disappointment.

However, the nature of the relationship between political and social upheaval and the Romantics was complex. Certainly, news of the French Revolution filled many with new hope for radical change. In London, Blake wore with pride the revolutionary colours, in defiance of official repression of revolutionary sympathy, and he was far from alone. William Wordsworth (1770–1850), looking back at his heady experiences of the time – he eagerly travelled to France to participate in the early days of the Revolution – wrote in 1850:

> But Europe at that time was filled with joy,
> France standing on the top of golden hours,
> And human nature seeming born again …
>
> (from *The Prelude* VI)

But as early optimism gave way to disillusion, the nature of Romanticism itself changed: in general, it manifested itself in less overtly political ways – although there were plenty of exceptions. Blake, for example, involved himself more and more in his own intricate mythologies and symbolic systems, although some critics have seen in these an attempt to retain radical, even revolutionary views but to express them in disguise so as to avoid the official censor. Other Romantic figures, such as Coleridge and Wordsworth, became more conservative as they saw the turn events were taking in France and Europe, characterised by the Terror and war. In part, this disillusion was born of personal disappointment: Wordsworth and Coleridge, inspired by egalitarian ideas, along with another poet Robert Southey (1774–1843), had invented a utopian scheme, which they called 'Pantisocracy', to set up an anarchistic commune on the banks of the Susquehanna in New England in 1794. However, for largely personal rather than ideological reasons, this scheme came to nothing, adding to the gathering sense of disillusion.

Another dominant characteristic of Romanticism, as already noted, was the emphasis on hero figures and heroic deeds. Often these were safely placed in the past, or in invented mythology, but post-revolutionary France was to give an inviting opportunity to focus on a real living hero figure. This was Napoleon Bonaparte, who made full use of the new political and social climate which recognised talent as opposed to birth and who rose rapidly through the ranks of the revolutionary army in its wars with counter-revolutionary European powers. So marked was his success that, in 1799, he became First Consul of France, the highest position in the new Republic. Artists such as Jacques-Louis David (1748–1825) and his pupil Antoine-Jean Gros (1771–1835) painted appropriately grandiose studies of Napoleon in heroic contexts. David went on to become Napoleon's official painter, cementing the role of the artist as Romantic propagandist. Elsewhere, the fiercely republican Beethoven dedicated his third symphony, the aptly titled *Eroica*, to Napoleon: 'The Great Symphony of Napoleon Bonaparte'. By the same token, however, Beethoven angrily removed this dedication on hearing the news that Napoleon had had himself crowned Emperor of France, substituting the far less personal 'heroic symphony composed to celebrate the memory of a great man'.

It is precisely this kind of angry denunciation, arising from deeply felt disillusion, that typified the reaction of many Romantics to the apparent failure of reality to live up to their imagined ideals. Indeed, it is possible to interpret the entire Romantic movement in terms of the failure of political and social revolution. David Blayney Brown, for instance, comments:

> Romanticism was born in opposition and sorrow, in social or national crisis and in individual trauma. Often associated with the

revolutionary spirit of the time, it was really the consequence of its failure – a compensating revolution in hearts and minds, an alternative empire of the imagination.

(from *Romanticism*, 2001)

Here there is great scope for individual interpretation of the spirit of Romanticism, based on a thorough exploration of the historical evidence – most importantly, the artistic creations of the Romantics themselves.

The social and economic contexts of Romanticism

War and revolution are especially dramatic examples of historical change, but other less dramatic contextual factors were also at work during this period, effecting profound and lasting social and economic changes in both Britain and Europe. Romanticism played its part here too, both as a symptom and as a factor in instigating these deep-seated changes. Crucially, the broadly Romantic period saw both economic expansion *and* hardship through the development of capitalism. The impact of war with France was hugely significant here, both as an important cause of economic changes, and as a factor in exacerbating the hardships of the dispossessed. Several further social changes made a deep mark on British society in this context. These included:

- rapidly accelerating population growth
- as a direct corollary of industrialisation, a general population drift from the countryside to the towns and cities
- vastly improving communications, especially with the coming of the railways and an efficient national postage service
- improving educational standards and increased literacy (of particular relevance to Romanticism).

Changes such as these provided fertile ground for the development of Romanticism, not least because of the socially unsettling effects of any swift and widespread changes in the way people live and behave. As the 18th century wore on, the essential tenets of the Neo-Classical outlook, with their emphasis on good order, good taste and rationality, began to seem hopelessly conservative and outdated. The artefacts of the Romantics, on the other hand, in literature, art and music, seemed to reflect the prevailing sense of and need for dramatic change.

The particular developments noted above facilitated the spread of new ideas, and it is worth exploring exactly how this happened. In some ways, it seems paradoxical that at the very time when material comfort and security were gaining ground, so too was dissatisfaction with their limitations. There may well be a parallel here with post-Second World War society in 20th-century Britain, especially during the 1960s. Marilyn Butler makes the point that:

> The most obvious feature common to all the arts of Western nations after 1750 was the refusal to validate the contemporary social world – even though to the retrospective eye those who lived in society were never so prosperous, powerful, or (presumably) happy. The art of the late Eighteenth Century fell decidedly out of love with material possessions … The strongest single tendency of late Eighteenth Century art was to reject the ephemeral in favour of the essential, and the search for purity often took the form of a journey into the remote.
>
> (from *Romantics, Rebels and Reactionaries*, 1981)

This may well have been true of the rapidly expanding professional and entrepreneurial middle classes. However, in a social system which was still very much hierarchical, hardship, degradation and misery were real enough for those unfortunate enough to live lower down the social scale. This too had its influence on Romanticism, even if merely as a reminder to those of educated sensibility that all things were not well. The French wars had an unprecedented impact here, as many able bodied labourers were recruited, with varying degrees of force, into the army and the navy and a high proportion of these became casualties of the battlefield or – even more prevalent – of disease. Those who survived in good health often found no jobs to go back to; there were severe economic recessions at intervals during the wars, and especially acute hardship after 1815, and well into the 1820s. For those who survived with injuries, there was no social security system, and miserable begging was often the only available occupation. The instability that inevitably accompanied rapid social change exacerbated the effects of war disastrously, in that village communities were no longer strong enough to cope. Marilyn Gaull has commented pertinently:

> The real victims of the war were, as always, the poor: in industry, overworked, taxed and hungry; in the countryside, dispossessed by increasing enclosures; in the army or navy, flogged and if they weren't killed, discharged, homeless and unrewarded, to a society that had no facilities for the infirm but the poorhouse or prison.
>
> (from *English Romanticism: The Human Context*, 1988)

When working people attempted to fight against this degradation, repression was swift: William Pitt's government, for example, passed the Combination Laws in

1799 and 1800, effectively prohibiting workers from combining in trade unions or other organisations as a means of working for better conditions. Repression after 1815 was even harsher, culminating in the Peterloo massacre of 1819, during which peaceful demonstrators in St Peter's Fields, Manchester, were slaughtered by cavalry.

The attitudes of writers and artists to the rural and urban poor were mixed. For many, the poor simply did not feature – in the novels of Jane Austen, for example, or the paintings of Constable. For others, the response tended to be personal rather than political or social, especially after the 1790s; Wordsworth's poems featuring the rural poor of the Lakes, for instance. But there were also some energetically radical responses, for example, Shelley's bitterly critical poem on the Peterloo massacre, 'The Mask of Anarchy – Written on the Occasion of the Massacre of Manchester', when, as he explained, 'the torrent of my indignation has not yet done boiling in my veins'. But then he was safely in Italy at the time.

Accompanying these changes, and very much part of them, was a dramatic expansion of economic markets into continents outside Europe – the growth of imperialism, in effect – and the exploitation of these new areas as a source of raw materials for the Industrial Revolution. The darkest side of this imperialist venture was the slave trade, and here Romantics played a significant part in leading opposition to slavery. The title of Hannah More's (1745–1833) poem, 'The Sorrows of Yamba, or the Negro Woman's Lamentation' (Part 3: Texts and extracts, page 71), speaks for itself. In many ways, this continuing opposition to slavery gave radical opinion a unity and focus well after the disillusion with revolutionary politics had set in. Blake, for example, implicitly acknowledged the horror of slavery in his poem 'The Little Black Boy', although, as it was included in the optimistically couched *Songs of Innocence* of 1789, there is here also a sense that the issue could, potentially at least, be harmoniously resolved. More explicitly, when William Turner exhibited his shockingly influential painting 'Slave Ship' in 1840, seven years after the slave trade had been officially abolished in the British Empire, there was still plenty of evidence of continuing slavery throughout the world. Turner's full title for the painting was 'Slavers throwing overboard the Dead and the Dying – Typhoon coming on', indicating the full horror of the depicted practice, and the accompanying inscription included the lines:

> Hope, Hope, fallacious Hope!
> Where is thy market now?'

It is possible to interpret the outrage against slavery, justifiable and ultimately effective though it was, as another sign of the fragmentation of radical thought – a failure of the radical nerve, in effect – within Romanticism. After all, the hardships of the rural and urban poor in Britain at that time were equally real, if less acute, and demanded an equally radical response. The anti-slavery movement, according to this interpretation, provided a relatively 'safe' outlet for radical indignation – concern at a distance, as it were – which may lend further credibility to a view of Romanticism emphasising its attraction to the exotic as opposed to realities closer to home. Here again the tension lies at the heart of any serious exploration of Romanticism and its expressions.

▶ Read 'The Sorrows of Yamba' (Part 3, page 71) and Blake's poem 'The Little Black Boy'. How effectively, in your view, does each poem make use of the first-person speaker to evoke a reaction from the reader?

Changing texts: making, distributing and consuming

Other social and economic changes, although less dramatic, also facilitated the development of Romanticism. The position of artists generally was one of increasing autonomy as the traditional system of aristocratic patronage began to wither away – although not without painful struggle – in favour of more market-led economics. Notable too was the transformation of the means of textual production and distribution, and accompanying this the rapid growth of a literate, educated section of the population eager for stimulating reading material. These changes were clearly part of industrialisation and urbanisation, in terms of both textual production and consumption. They affected other art forms too – sheet music sold widely for domestic use, regular theatre and concert going became a feature of middle class life, and paintings were needed to decorate the new urban villas – but they were particularly stimulating of literary expansion.

Throughout the Romantic period, poetry remained the most literary and academically prestigious form of the written word. Indeed, as a distillation of language along rhythmic and symbolic lines, it has a special place as the Romantic art form *par excellence*. But other literary forms also made their mark during this period, notably the novel, aided by an enthusiastic readership with increased leisure in which to read, relatively cheap mechanised print-runs, and the development of subscription-based circulating libraries such as the Minerva Press Library, established in London in 1773. In this context, the position of middle-class women was especially important, signifying a growing female confidence and independence based on greater educational opportunities on the one hand, and, on the other, increased leisure time as wives and daughters unable to enter the professions or even find much by way of meaningful work. Female novelists like Jane Austen, Ann Radcliffe, Mary Shelley and, later, the Brontë sisters blazed a trail for future generations and helped to lay the foundations for the literary prestige enjoyed by the novel today.

In effect, as David Punter asserts, 'the whole economic base of literature changed' (from 'Romantics to Early Victorians' in *The Romantic Age in Britain*, ed. Boris Ford, 1992). And not only literature. During this period, newspapers and periodicals expanded greatly in the range available and in size of readership. Mechanisation played a crucial role here too – *The Times*, for example, adopted steam-driven printing machinery in 1814 – and the rapidly developing railway network ensured efficient distribution. In some ways, all this helped to cement class distinctions, in that different journals had very specific class-based readerships in mind. In other respects, though, improving literacy levels, more concentrated urban populations and the relative cheapness of newspapers led to British society becoming more of a homogeneous reading public. In 1816, for example, William Cobbett (1763–1835) established the first British cheap periodical, *The Political Register*, which did a great deal to spread his radical message and, incidentally, to help identify Romanticism with political radicalism.

Higher up the social scale, the journals tended to be less overtly political – perhaps because the upper-class and upper middle-class audience, holding power anyway, felt no need to prove a point. But here too, there was considerable influence on the growth of Romanticism in the dissemination of artistic and cultural knowledge and opinion through reviews, which became increasingly influential as arbiters of taste. Conversely, reviews implying 'good taste' also gave the more subversive and innovative of the Romantics something to struggle against – William Blake being a case in point here. One way or another, journals such as the *Edinburgh Magazine* (1802), the *Quarterly Review* (1809), and *Blackwood's Magazine* (1817) played an important part, not least in ensuring that the arts, generally, were seen as central to social life. Further, they provided an important platform for a new breed of polemical, cultured and influential writers and thinkers like William Hazlitt (1778–1830), Leigh Hunt (1784–1859) and Thomas de Quincey (1785–1859), who moved in Romantic circles and who were instrumental in crystallising and spreading the appropriate values.

The spiritual contexts of Romanticism

In his essay 'Romanticism and Classicism', the philosopher T.E. Hulme (1883–1917) used a telling phrase when he described Romanticism as 'spilt religion'. He intended this in a disparaging sense, and he had his own agenda – as of course do all writers – in reacting against what he saw as the excesses of late Romanticism, in favour of the 'hard dry image' of Imagism, the school of poetry he helped to establish before the First World War. However, it is worth exploring the metaphor of 'spilt religion' a little further, to see if it may yield a more positive image of Romanticism.

'Spilt' implies something messy, something not quite in the right place, the result perhaps of some accidental, unjudged movement. But it could also imply the result of some new entity displacing – spilling – the original contents. If religion is taken to be one of the positive characteristics of being human, a 'pure' entity, its spillage is something to be avoided. Yet all these points could be turned on their head, even celebrated, by a Romantic outlook. After all, why should something as powerful as the religious impulse be safely contained in some kind of receptacle? At least if one spills something, it implies that the substance might actually be used rather than simply kept safely intact. And the spillage itself – might that not also form an attractive pattern? Perhaps there are some helpful pointers here towards a fuller understanding of the spiritual nature and contexts of Romanticism.

Amidst these interpretive possibilities one thing is certain: the Romantic period was characterised by intense spiritual confusion and seeking. There was a mounting challenge to the privileged position of the 'official' Christianity of the Church of England. The growth of rationalism and empiricism – basing all ideas on tangible evidence – during the Enlightenment had doubtless led to a devaluation of religious experience in any immediate sense. In the mid-18th century, the vast majority of educated people broadly accepted Christian beliefs and morality, but saw little reason to go beyond this. Romanticism challenged this conventional stability through its restoration of spiritual experience to the centre of human concerns. Literature assumed a special place in this process, especially in Britain and Germany, where it tended to fill the vacuum left by the decline of orthodox belief, and simultaneously to appropriate some of the language and symbolic systems of religion. Thus M.H. Abrams, an influential critic on Romanticism, has called literature 'reconstituted theology', a 'secularised form of devotional experience' (quoted in Marilyn Gaull *English Romanticism*, 1988). Romantic literature, as with other art forms, was frequently intimately confessional, in a strongly autobiographical sense, emphasising the uniqueness of individual experience through the use of the imagination. In this respect, art itself, in the broadest sense, became the means to an end of spiritual fulfilment in a way that was totally unprecedented.

The key word here is 'imagination'. Writers such as Blake and Coleridge saw the imagination as the visionary faculty, enabling spiritual insight into ultimate truth. Creative art was the imagination truly at work – and play. Blake made this claim in his own 'Descriptive Catalogue' for *The Vision of the Last Judgement* (1810), focusing on the use of images (and the semantic similarity of image and imagination is helpful here):

If the spectator could enter into these images in his imagination, if he ... could make a friend and companion of one of these images of wonder ... then would he arise from his grave, then would he meet the Lord in the air and then would he be happy. General knowledge is remote knowledge; it is in particulars that wisdom consists and happiness too.

Elsewhere he referred to 'the true vine of eternity, the human imagination'. In this conception, the images and symbols are provided by nature, and are often steeped in implied religious meaning accrued over the ages, but are transformed by the imagination. Blake acknowledged that 'it is impossible to think without images of somewhat on earth', but these images become powerfully and meaningfully human only when they enter consciousness. Coleridge echoed these sentiments in his *Biographia Literaria* (1817), speaking of

> ... the primary IMAGINATION as the living Power and prime Agent of all human Perception ... a repetition in the finite mind of the eternal act of creation in the infinite I AM.

For August Schlegel, from whom Coleridge borrowed and developed many ideas, beauty itself was 'a symbolic representation of the infinite' (Berlin lectures, 1801–1802). A sense of mysterious beauty became an intrinsic part of Romantic art, embodying philosophical speculations like these. As William Hazlitt observed in his aptly titled treatise *Why Distant Objects Please* (1821–1822), 'We drink the air before us, and borrow a more refined existence from objects that hover on the brink of nothingness.' The religious connotations could scarcely be clearer.

Although there was a great deal of common ground in the spirituality of the Romantics, there were many important differences. Romantics' relationships to Christianity were diverse, and often indicative of personal stories and wider philosophical outlooks – hardly surprising given the long-standing traditional power of the Chritian religion. True, as David Blayney Brown maintains:

> It was ... the punitive concept of original sin (the idea that humans are born sinful) that alienated many Romantics from conventional Christianity. Its moral code of self-denial was incompatible with their aim of self-fulfilment.
>
> (from *Romanticism*, 2001)

But even this relatively common ground could be unstable. William Blake remained a Christian throughout his life, but a highly unorthodox one, seeing Christ as an embodiment of the imagination rebelling against any imposed external authority. In his very unorthodoxy, Blake was part of the dissenting tradition in British Christianity, emphasising the authority of personal vision as opposed to the social structures of any established church. Blake's family had been involved in the radically mystical Swedenborgian Church, but even this highly unorthodox form of Christianity proved too conformist for Blake, and his book *The Marriage of Heaven and Hell* can be read as a spirited critique of the Swedenborgian position. Blake took non-conformity to an extreme, proclaiming through his character Los in *Jerusalem*:

> I must create a system or be enslaved by another man's.
> I will not reason or compare: my business is to create.

But even, or perhaps especially, in this he continued to represent the individualistic, unorthodox, dissenting wing of Protestantism. This was a very powerful influence on Romanticism, and one reason why it took root so firmly in Britain and northern Germany – both intensely Protestant.

Coleridge, on the other hand, left his radical version of Christianity behind as he grew older. There is a sense in which his life and work reflected an inner struggle between radical spirituality and orthodox Christian belief – and in this he typified many of his day. In 'The Eeolian Harp' of 1795, for example, he characterises his wife, Sara, as reproving him for wandering – wondering, even – too far from conventional codes of belief:

> But thy more serious eye a mild reproof
> Darts, O beloved Woman! nor such thoughts
> Dim and unhallow'd dost thou not reject
> And biddest me walk humbly with my God.
> Meek Daughter in the family of Christ!

In his youth, pulled towards poetic, spiritual and political radicalism – as exemplified in the Pantisocratic venture (see page 23) – the subversive, adventurous side of his character was in the ascendant. However, it was the conservative nature, ultimately, of his religious outlook that spelled the end of his radicalism. By 1817, in his second 'Lay Sermon' he was espousing a conservative view of the role of religion, as a bulwark of the state through the established Church of England: 'To the feudal system we owe the *forms*, to the Church the *substance* of our liberty.' Wordsworth and others (the eventual poet laureate Robert Southey for example) took similar paths towards conservatism, whilst others still – particularly the next generation of Romantics, Shelley, Keats and Byron among them – explored ever more radical spiritual paths, including outright atheism and paganism. The diverging routes may be seen in this vivid recollection by Benjamin Haydon of the young Keats, virtually unknown and experimenting enthusiastically in his poetry and beliefs, reading his verse to the acclaimed 'great poet' of the establishment, Wordsworth, in 1817:

Wordsworth received him kindly, & after a few minutes, Wordsworth asked him what he had been lately doing. I said he has just finished an exquisite ode to Pan – and as he had not a copy I begged Keats to repeat it – which he did in his usual half chant, (most touching) walking up and down the room – when he had done I felt really, as if I had heard a young Apollo – Wordsworth drily said 'a very pretty piece of Paganism' – This was unfeeling, & unworthy of his high Genius to a young Worshipper like Keats – & Keats felt it deeply.

This recollection gives a good idea of the flavour of events like this, particularly the highly serious attitude towards the art of poetry. Ultimately, despite the many differences of approach and the conflicts which divided several of the individuals involved, it is possible to agree with Hugh Honour that 'The Romantics believed with St Paul that "the letter killeth but the spirit giveth life".' And it seems appropriate that this too is a centrally Christian formulation.

Romantic feminism and femininity

Throughout the upheaval that was Romanticism, one half of the population remained subservient to the other: men continued to dominate women in all walks of life, and by and large seemed determined to prolong this arrangement. However, this is only part of the story, for during the same period it is possible to discern the beginnings of the movement towards female liberation – feminism, in effect – through the agency of particularly strong-minded and intellectually robust women, not least in the field of literature. At the same time, it became more possible for men to acknowledge and even welcome aspects of what might be traditionally called femininity, both in themselves and in social – particularly familial – arrangements. The Romantic emphasis on sensibility may be seen in this light, as a way of liberating 'feminine' aspects of the male psyche, at the very moment that women began to demand and struggle for a fairer slice of the patriarchal cake. On the other hand, from a radical feminist viewpoint, such acknowledgements of femininity in the male may be seen as simply another, subtly employed, way of increasing masculine power. Anne Mellor, for example, in her ground-breaking book *Romanticism and Gender* (1993) has described the Romantic (male) appropriation of femininity in these terms:

By taking on the feminine virtues of compassion, mercy, gentleness and sympathy, the male Romantic poets could claim to speak with ultimate moral as well as intellectual authority … By usurping the mother's womb, life-giving power, and feminine sensibilities, the male poet could claim to be God, the sole ruler of the world.

The relationships between these rather different characteristics of the Romantic age manifested themselves in the artistic endeavours of both women and men (including some of the texts featured in this book) in sometimes contradictory, sometimes complementary ways. The resulting tensions often gave rise to stimulating and vivid artistic forms.

Mary Wollstonecraft

Romanticism, as has already been noted, had a fondness for hero figures. In the case of Romantic feminism – or at least its brave, embattled beginnings – the hero was a heroine, appropriately enough: Mary Wollstonecraft (1759–1797). It would be hard to over-estimate her importance. Her influence took many forms: through her prolific writings, avidly read and followed by a growing readership – in particular, her seminal work *A Vindication of the Rights of Woman* (1792); through her circle of friends and associates, including political radicals and creative artists; through her educational work, culminating in her 'plan for education' (1793) at the invitation of the revolutionary French government; through her marriage to William Godwin, a radical anarchist thinker and writer; and through the product of this marriage, the child Mary who would become Mary Shelley after marrying the poet Shelley (and under this name be known to posterity as the author of *Frankenstein*). Sadly, Mary Wollstonecraft died of complications arising from her pregnancy, at the relatively tender age of 37 – it is all the more astounding that she achieved so much in such a short lifetime.

Thomas Paine's hugely significant book *The Rights of Man* (1791), itself a riposte to Edmund Burke's counter-revolutionary treatise *Reflections on the Revolution in France* (1790), had been shocking enough, but at least the central idea of men having some sort of rights was fairly prevalent – it was more the extent and limits of these rights that was debated. But there was an altogether different response to Mary Wollstonecraft's book on the rights of women, following as it did her educationally radical *Thoughts on the Education of Daughters* (1787). Wollstonecraft called for equality for women in education, the professions, the law, and in politics. The book was hugely successful, and by 1796 had reached its third edition, with a French translation as well. The very idea that it was possible to think of women having rights at all was outrageous to dominant male intellectual opinion in the late 18th century. Horace Walpole (1717–1797), a writer of some importance in the development of the gothic novel, especially with *The Castle of Otranto* (1764), reviled Wollstonecraft as a 'hyena in petticoats' for her radical feminism. Incredible as it may seem, her effigy was publicly burned at the time. Wollstonecraft's own life is fascinating in itself, not simply as a powerful influence on feminist thought. She was a fierce and wide-ranging critic of all forms of oppression, including the contemporary version of marriage whereby women were virtually owned by their husbands as replacements for their similarly proprietorial fathers. And yet she eventually fell in love with and married William Godwin, himself a radical dissenter from conventional views on marriage, in a spirit of equal partnership and mutual, respectful affection. In many ways, she fits the bill for the romantic and Romantic heroine – feminine and feminist in a way that strikes a chord in the 21st century: strongly individualistic, passionate, well travelled, experienced in (and profoundly hurt by) relationships with men, and with 'a smile of bewitching tenderness' in the words of Godwin himself in his *Memoirs*.

Mary Warnock, in her fascinating survey *Woman Philosophers* (1996), refers specifically to Wollstonecraft's central publication, adding 'it is perhaps from 1792 that one can date a specific feminist "movement", with a determination amongst free-thinking women to unite to claim their rights'. This is quite a claim, and testifies to a powerful contextual influence in the development of Romanticism. Key dates and key figures are often highly significant, but clearly there needs also to be fertile ground. Here again, the world – or at least Western Europe – was just about ready for the advent of embryonic feminism. As Claire Tomalin, in her 1974 biography of Wollstonecraft, put it: 'Mary Wollstonecraft took up her pen at the moment when the great wave of Enlightenment thinking, with its questioning of the institutions of religion, monarchy, **patriarchy** and slavery, was moving clearly towards a revised view of the position of women.' So when Wollstonecraft wrote of men's absurd expectations of women in her 'portrait of a house slave', she was to some extent reflecting the spirit of the age:

> Such a woman ought to be an angel – or she is an ass – for I discern not a trace of the human character, neither reason nor passion in this domestic drudge, whose being is absorbed in that of a tyrant's.

Despite these new stirrings of awareness by women, in the patriarchal society of the day it needed influential men to help disseminate the message. One of the most important of these was Wollstonecraft's close friend and publisher, Joseph Johnson (1738–1809). Johnson was hugely influential both as a publisher – aside from Wollstonecraft, he published works by such key figures as Blake, Paine, Godwin, Wordsworth and Coleridge – and as a giver of regular dinners in the rooms above his office at St Paul's Churchyard in London for his like-minded radical friends. These dinners became significant forums for ideas and discussion, and for meeting during potentially dangerous times – although Johnson was himself imprisoned for six months in 1798 for selling a seditious pamphlet. At one of these gatherings, Wollstonecraft met Paine for the first time, and was inspired by his revolutionary ideas. At another, she met Blake, who went on to illustrate some of her children's stories, and who may have been directly influenced by Wollstonecraft's ideas on the slavery of women in his *Visions of the Daughters of Albion* (1793):

> Till she who burns with youth, and knows no fixed lot, is bound
> In spells of law to one she loaths: and must she drag the chain
> Of life, in weary lust! must chilling murderous thoughts obscure
> The clear heaven of her eternal spring?

Other important female writers and thinkers followed Wollstonecraft, influenced by her and by the climate of radical opinion. Notable here were Helen Maria Williams (1762–1827), who wrote enthusiastically of the French experience in her 'Letters from France' (1792); Charlotte Smith (1748–1806), whose novel *The Old Manor House* (1793) may be read – and certainly was at the time – as a fictional critique of patriarchy; and, in the longer term, Wollstonecraft's own daughter Mary Shelley (1797–1851), whose *Frankenstein* may convincingly be read in the same way.

A new wave of women writers

In other ways, as has already been noted, the arts both reflected and influenced changing ideas and the changing roles of women. The growth and development of the novel was perhaps the most indicative of this inter-relationship, in that it provided an opportunity, as a relatively new literary form of growing but still relatively low status, for active female involvement, both as writers and readers. In the earlier part of the 18th century, male novelists tended to portray female characters in stereotypically subservient ways: the innocent, unquestioningly obedient Sophia in Fielding's *Tom Jones* (1749); the mean-spirited, bitter Tabitha in Smollett's *Humphrey Clinker* (1771); the passive, malleable victim Clarissa in Richardson's novel of that name (1748), for example. But with a new wave of women writers, the situation changed dramatically. They included Fanny Burney (1752–1840), who in her novels *Cecilia* (1782) and *Camilla* (1796) explored the relationship between active women and their social contexts, and Jane Austen (1775–1817), who was influenced by Burney and who went on to satirise relentlessly the patriarchal society she found herself in. Such skilled exponents of the novelist's art prepared the ground for the further achievements of the Brontë sisters, Charlotte (1816–1855), Emily (1818–1848) and Anne (1820–1849), as David Punter has noted, in *The Romantic Age in Britain* (1992):

> With the Brontës, we see women writers moving into and authoritatively claiming a different area, the area of passion and desire. Here the achievement is twofold: on the one hand there is the detailed exploration of the female psyche itself, on the other there is the provision of a set of male characters who are clearly conjured not from outdated male myths of heroism but rather from female

fantasy, and who are therefore enduringly fraught with the ambivalence which is latent within the whole notion of the hero from the gothic writers on.

The idea, subtly presented by female writers who in many ways were socially conventional, that men could be manipulated by women, often by playing on their sensitive feminine sides, is an abiding testimony to Romanticism.

▶ In the light of modern ideas on gender relationships, often focusing on the role of the 'new man' and the tensions involved for both sexes in making adjustments from more traditional formulations of gender, consider the relevance of Romanticism today. In particular, it may be fruitful to evaluate notions of 'femininity' and 'feminism', asking whether they both have roots in Romantic attitudes and to what extent they are either contradictory or complementary.

Innocence and experience in Romanticism

Closely linked to ideas about feminism and femininity were speculations centring on the nature of innocence and experience. Traditionally, childhood, if seen as separate from maturity at all, was viewed simply as a means to an end – a preparation for adulthood during which corrective measures were the order of the day. For the bulk of the population, of course, this was more or less a matter of economic necessity: as in much of the world today, children were another method of helping, often precariously, to make ends meet. This applied equally to the countryside and the rapidly expanding urban areas. Coupled with economic hardship was a high infant mortality rate; indeed the two were often linked – overworked, underfed children were unlikely to survive into adulthood. Under these circumstances, it would have been foolish for parents to make too great an emotional investment in their offspring, for fear of savage disappointment lying in wait. The theological doctrine of original sin, embedded in official Christianity, served to justify a negative view of childhood: experience was valued above innocence in alleviating the effects of sinfulness.

However, for the Romantics a new vision of innocence gained ground, in which the sense of wonder in childhood was valued as being similar to the sense of newness essential to imaginative creativity at any age. The German Romantic poet and philosopher Friedrich Schiller (1759–1805), whose 'An die Freude' ('Ode to Joy') would form the basis of the final movement of Beethoven's quintessentially Romantic 9th Symphony, wrote enthusiastically of the need for adults to rediscover childhood perceptions through the deliberate and conscious cultivation of play:

> For, to declare it once and for all, Man plays only when he is, in the full meaning of the word, Man, and is only wholly Man, when at play.

The artist Samuel Palmer (1805–1881) wrote of his 'childlike sense of wonder' as a pre-requisite of inspired art. For enlightened thinkers, education began to be seen more in terms of carefully nurturing child-like sensibilities than in simply inculcating correct models of behaviour through sanctions of varying degrees of harshness. Whereas economic hardship contributed tellingly towards a view of childhood, which at best ignored it and at worst exploited it, as a malleable form of labour, by the same token economic prosperity at least allowed for a more tolerant, indulgent model of childhood. In this respect, circumstances favoured the Romantics, in that for the more enlightened and progressive sections of the middle and upper classes – including many of the key figures of Romanticism – desperate economic want had been banished.

As with so much else in the history of Romanticism, it would be misleading to see the development of new conceptions of childhood and the state of innocence purely in terms of a sudden break from the past. Throughout the 18th century there had been a gathering sense of the value of childhood as a state of being essentially different from adulthood: in effect, the invention of childhood. This shift in opinion itself drew on earlier traditions – celebrated, for example, in branches of radical Christianity and expressed in the poetry and prose of such 17th-century writers as Thomas Traherne (1637–1674) and Henry Vaughan (1621–1695). Traherne, for example, wrote of his own childhood visions in *The Centuries* (c.1637):

> All appeared new, and strange at first, inexpressibly rare and delightful and beautiful. I was a little stranger, which at my entrance into the world was saluted and surrounded with innumerable joys. My knowledge was divine.
>
> (Third *Century*, section 2)

By the time William Blake assembled his *Songs of Innocence* – one of the first and fullest expressions of a Romantic position on childhood innocence – the tradition of celebrating the visions of childhood had become diluted through its use of platitudes, and was in danger of drowning in over-sentimentality. It may be argued that Blake and similar thinkers were not so much inventing something new as restoring a certain robust, relevant and invigorating quality in an already established tradition. Certainly, this was the way that many Romantics themselves saw their stance – innovative principally in order to recover true, time-honoured values which were in danger of being lost to modern beliefs in the power of reason and science. The spirit of Romanticism placed the notion of childhood innocence at its very centre. And nowhere is this more apparent than in the work of Blake.

William Blake – innocence and experience

William Blake made his intentions abundantly clear in the introductory frontispiece to his aptly titled *Songs of Innocence* (1789): to liberate adult consciousness through a recovery of the key characteristics of innocence. The illustration depicts an adult shepherd with his pipe, clearly led and inspired by the winged infant above him. Blake was also working in the tradition of writing verse for a childhood readership – indeed the Romantic era saw a huge increase in the number of texts published for children. The 'Songs' are both for and about children, and cluster round what Blake saw as the liberating imaginative power and truthfulness of the state of innocence, as encapsulated in his later poem, 'Auguries of Innocence':

> To see a world in a grain of sand
> And a heaven in a wild flower,
> Hold infinity in the palm of your hand
> And eternity in an hour.

In the 'Introduction' to the *Songs of Innocence*, Blake seems to characterise himself, the creative poet, as a piper, then a singer, and finally as a writer – each in turn inspired by the swiftly passing, ephemeral wishes of a laughing child as muse:

> Piping down the valleys wild
> Piping songs of pleasant glee
> On a cloud I saw a child
> And he laughing said to me
>
> Pipe a song about a lamb
> So I piped with merry cheer
> Piper pipe that song again
> So I piped; he wept to hear.
>
> Drop thy pipe thy happy pipe
> Sing thy songs of happy cheer
> So I sung the same again
> While he wept with joy to hear.
>
> Piper sit thee down and write
> In a book that all may read –
> So he vanished from my sight
> And I plucked a hollow reed

And I made a rural pen
And I stained the water clear
And I wrote my happy songs
Every child may joy to hear.

It is possible to read this apparently simple introductory poem as a sort of manifesto of the role of the Romantic poet: aiming at writing inspired by and intended to refresh the spirit of innocence, and seeking to capture the fleeting moment of imaginative vision. In a sense the remaining poems in the *Songs of Innocence* collection say much the same thing, but in a lively array of settings, viewpoints and narrative contexts. Some are tinged with sadness, fear, anger and loss – Blake knew full well that these qualities are as much part of innocence as is carefree, joyful enthusiasm. Yet there is throughout the collection a pervading sense of optimistic, harmonious resolution of any conflict. Such is the poet's power with his 'rural pen'. An observant, subtle reading of this poem, however, may uncover a slight sense of doubt here, characteristic of Blake's robust intellectual honesty: the rural pen 'stained the water clear', perhaps suggesting a sullying of the purity of the original moment. It may well be that Blake, the archetypal Romantic inspired poet, was aware from his earliest work of the limitations – even ambivalence – of his verbal art. Nevertheless, language is the most effective tool known to humankind and as such must be made to work for the spirit of imagination: this appears to be the central message.

Ambivalence about the nature of innocence in the context of a harsh, exploitative world – even while celebrating its vitality and engaging force – becomes more marked when the *Songs of Innocence* are read alongside their counterparts in what would become *Songs of Innocence and of Experience* (1794). The idea of writing a complementary, or contrasting, set of poems dealing with experience seems to have come to Blake fairly soon after the publication of *Songs of Innocence* in 1789, and there is evidence that he was working on the new poems in the early 1790s. Certainly the two 'states of the human soul', as Blake subtitled the 1794 edition, were very closely – perhaps inextricably – linked in Blake's mind. It would be simplistic indeed to read innocence as good and experience as bad; the thrust of the poems is far more subtle and unsettling than that – even, as has been noted, in the apparently entirely cheerful 'Introduction' to *Innocence*. Nevertheless, the two dates of publication, 1789 and 1794, could well indicate a certain onset of disillusion with the effectiveness of innocence alone in a corrupt and hostile world. Of course 1789 was the year of the French Revolution, which Blake welcomed enthusiastically; by 1794 the harsh reality of the Terror had caused widespread disillusion. Interesting here is the sense that the concepts of innocence and experience, far from relating simply to the needs of children, may be seen in context as vital to the spirit of Romanticism.

Brief examination of the two poems entitled 'Nurse's Song' – one in the *Innocence* section, the other in *Experience*, as printed below, may serve to highlight further some of the issues and ambivalences here.

Nurse's Song
(*Innocence* version)

When the voices of children are heard on the green,
And laughing is heard on the hill,
My heart is at rest within my breast
And everything else is still.

Then come home my children: the sun is gone down
And the dews of night arise.
Come, leave off play and let us away,
Till the morning appears in the skies.

No let us play for it is yet day
And we cannot go to sleep.
Besides in the sky the little birds fly,
And the hills are all covered in sheep.

Well well go and play till the light fades away
And then go home to bed
The little ones leaped and shouted and laughed
And all the hills echoed.

Nurse's Song
(*Experience* version)

When the voices of children are heard on the green,
And whisperings are in the dale,
The days of my youth rise fresh in my mind,
My face turns green and pale.

Then come home my children: the sun is gone down
And the dews of night arise.
Your spring and your day are wasted in play,
And your winter and night in disguise.

The nuances of meaning differentiating innocence from experience derive from the interplay and contrast between the two poems. In the *Innocence* version, the children's nurse, representing a form of adult consciousness, is guided by their wishes: she allows them to carry on playing until tiredness sets in. Crucially, she allows dialogue to unfold, enabling innocence – the children at play – and her own experience to complement each other harmoniously.

In the *Experience* version, however, there is no such dialogue: the nurse is the only speaker, and she seems embittered in her view of childhood innocence and, pertinently, of the innocent side of her own personality. The setting seems identical, as signified by the first line, but this adult's view then colours the picture according to her own unhappy memories. Rather than celebrating the sounds of play as the innocent nurse did – 'laughing is heard on the hill' – in terms of openness, this adult infers guilt and secrecy from the scene: 'whisperings are in the dale'. Her own youth and its sufferings recalled, this nurse seeks to inflict the same sort of limitations on the new generation – whereas the force of innocence seeks to break this vicious circle. The opening of the second stanza again echoes the *Innocence* version, but the closing two lines of the *Experience* poem are the most sinister of all, suggesting cold, dark secrecy and that enigmatic reference to 'disguise'. Certainly, Blake was writing within an already established pastoral tradition where 'innocence' had virtually become a cliché; his version of innocence, on the other hand, was anything but merely decorative or cloyingly sentimental. In an important sense, he was attempting to transform the meaning and status of innocence through the power of his poetry, and this connects Blake strongly to Romanticism in general.

Rousseau – radical education

Another key figure in the forming of Romantic attitudes to childhood and innocence was the Swiss philosopher Jean-Jacques Rousseau (1712–1778), despite the fact that his dates prefigured the Romantic era as commonly understood. In many respects, Rousseau can be seen as something of an antithesis to Blake: his chief medium was philosophical prose, whereas Blake gloried in imaginative verse; Rousseau emphasised the need for careful social planning – even social engineering – while Blake valued intuitive individual inspiration above all. Nevertheless, in the context of the development of 18th-century thought, informing Romanticism, the two may be seen as complementary figures, and both ended up saying much the same thing about the value of childhood and child-like qualities. Rousseau analysed the ills of contemporary society as stemming from a divorce between civilisation and the original, innocent state of nature – a state he saw as fundamentally benign. Realising that any return to such a state would be impossible, he concentrated his energies on education, seeing childhood development as continually replaying – in microcosm, as it were – the change from nature to civilisation. In *Emile* (1762), Rousseau elaborated on his educational principles, weaving philosophy into evocative fiction to establish the principles for an educational system embodying humane values – at least for boys, as his radical ideas failed to extend to girls and women. Essentially, he saw the necessity of allowing full scope for the individual development of the child in surroundings as natural as possible, protected by benign adults from the harmful influences of society, and fostering resourceful, independent and ethical characteristics. Perhaps rather perversely, the potentially harmful influences included books; only after reaching the age of 12 is Emile allowed to read one book: Defoe's *Robinson Crusoe*.

Interestingly, in the light of this observation, the position of English as a subject on the modern school and university curricula is largely because of Romantic – often Rousseauesque – developments in educational thought and practice in the 19th and 20th centuries. English, especially in terms of personal imaginative growth in childhood and as contact with the literary heritage, would eventually be seen as a great civilising, and even spiritual, force within the schooling system. As a modern educational writer, Peter Abbs, has observed, 'The roots of English lie in the tougher side of the Romantic movement.'

In the same year as *Emile* became available, 1762, Rousseau published his *Du Contrat Social* ('The Social Contract'), extrapolating from his theories on childhood and education to establish a radical political, democratic position. This was to be hugely influential on both European and American revolutionary politics. The famous opening lines of *Du Contrat Social* proclaim 'Man is born free, and everywhere he is in chains.' Essentially, however, Rousseau saw the need to exchange something of the freedom of original innocence for a harmonious social contract, while never losing sight of fundamental, natural values as a way of holding civilisation – Blake's 'experience', in effect – to account:

> The passing from the state of nature to the civil society produces a remarkable change in man; it puts justice as a rule of conduct in the place of instinct, and gives his actions the moral quality they previously lacked. ... And although in civil society man surrenders some of the advantages that belong to the state of nature, he gains in return far greater ones; his faculties are so exercised and developed, his mind is so enlarged, his sentiments so ennobled, and his whole spirit so elevated, that, if the abuse of his new condition did not in many cases lower him to something worse than what he had left, he should constantly bless the happy hour that lifted him forever from the state of nature and from a stupid, limited animal made a creature of intelligence and a man.
>
> (from *The Social Contract*, 1762)

Above all, when considering the social context of Romanticism, it is important to bear in mind the balanced, essentially civilised nature of such a conception of society, both actual and potential, as shared by Blake and Rousseau and deriving from ideas on the fundamental innocence of humanity.

▶ In many respects the modern education system is greatly indebted to Romantic notions about the value of innocence, and of learning through actual experience ('experiential learning', as this is sometimes called). There is a constant tension between this sort of child-centred approach and an alternative view emphasising didactic (teacher-led) transmission of knowledge, strict discipline, and rigorous testing. It may be appropriate, having read about Romantic notions of innocence, to evaluate and discuss your own experiences of schooling to judge how far Romantic attitudes prevail.

The range of Romantic art forms

The power of music

Blake and Rousseau, along with most other Romantics, saw value in play – and in an important sense, the arts could be seen as the adult version of play. As such, strict formal boundaries both within and between the various art forms tended to be eroded – another instance of the reaction to what was increasingly perceived as narrow Classicism. The merging of and interplay between the arts was increasingly widespread, and was seen as a positive virtue. To take the two key figures just examined as examples, Blake skilfully combined art and poetry in his work, based on his training as an engraver, and according to eyewitness accounts sang many of his poems to a select audience. Rousseau was also a keen musician, experimenting with opera, as well as writing fictional and non-fictional prose and drama. It is perhaps no accident that, despite the reputation that both men have gained as writers, and despite the emphasis of this book on textual forms of Romanticism, it is an interest in music that links them.

The power of music began to be recognised as somehow purer, less mediated and adulterated, than other art forms during the Romantic era. Musicians and composers began to throw off the yoke of servitude and aristocratic patronage (they had been little more than liveried servants for centuries) in favour of greater artistic, professional and personal autonomy – although this was certainly not a straightforward development without painful struggle and, all too often, abject poverty.

Even a cursory look at what some contemporaries said about the power of music serves to underline its growing significance. Schiller pronounced the validity of other art forms, pictorial and textual, as relative to the power of music: 'the plastic arts, at their most perfect, must become music. ... Poetry, when most fully developed, must grip us as powerfully as music does ...' (from *On the Aesthetic Education of Man*, 1795). The composer and music critic, Ernst Hoffman (1776–1822), echoed these sentiments in his appraisal of the music of Beethoven (1810); for him it 'sets in motion the lever of fear, of awe, of horror, of suffering, and awakens that infinite longing which is the essence of Romanticism'.

Beethoven himself was keenly conscious of the nature of his genius, seeing his musical powers as a gift – if sometimes a malign one – from a divine source. He was reported in 1810 to have told Elizabeth Brentano, a beautiful and cultured admirer, that

> ... when I open my eyes I must sigh, for what I see is contrary to my religion, and I must despise the world which does not know that music is a higher revelation than all wisdom and philosophy, the wine which inspires one to new generative processes, and I am the Bacchus who presses out the glorious wine for mankind and makes them spiritually drunken. ... Music is the one incorporeal entrance into the higher world of knowledge which comprehends mankind but which mankind cannot comprehend.

The reliability of this witness has been questioned, and when Beethoven saw her record of the conversation he exclaimed, 'Did I say that? Well, then I had a raptus!' In a sense, of course, it does not matter whether he said these words or not; the sentiments typify the gathering Romantic attitudes to music and to the spiritual among both musicians and their audiences. For Beethoven, music was a direct representation of spiritual feeling, and that was its whole point. Writing, on the other hand, caused him often to stumble incoherently: apologising for a delay in answering a letter from a friend, he wrote, 'I often compose the answer in my mind, but when I wish to write it down, I usually throw the pen away, because I cannot write as I feel.' The German composer, Felix Mendelssohn (1809–1847), developed this crucial distinction between writing and music:

> What any music I like expresses for me is not *thoughts too indefinite* to clothe in words, but *too definite*. – If you asked me what I thought on the occasion in question, I say, the song itself precisely as it stands. And if, in this or that instance, I had in my mind a definite word or definite words, I would not utter them to a soul, because words do not mean for one person what they mean for another; because the song alone can say to one, can awake in him, the same feelings it can in another – feelings, however, not to be expressed by the same words.

Interesting, if controversial, here is the sense of music as being more explicit in conveying meaning than text – an explicitness that could lead directly to a sense of a community of feeling rather more easily than with text. Reading, after all, must remain a fairly private activity. The statement also links interestingly with Romantic ideas about the education of feeling in children, as professed by Blake and Rousseau amongst others, in the sense that music seems to pre-date verbal language in its appeal to the senses.

It may also be true that, of all the art forms, it is music that has the most universal appeal. It is rare indeed to encounter someone for whom all forms of music are unattractive or uninteresting, but one could not say this about art, dance, novels, drama or poetry. However, it is important to realise that for the Romantics, music rarely stood alone: in many ways it is the cross-fertilisation of art forms and genres that was most significant in the development of the Romantic aesthetic sense. Thus, poetry, with its strong rhythmic sense and relatively smooth transformation into melody, was celebrated as the textual form above others. The Austrian Romantic composer Franz Schubert (1797–1828), especially, achieved a great deal in his tragically short life in bringing poetry and music together in his *lieder*, or lyrical songs.

Pictorial art and artists

There were also strong links between the pictorial arts and other art forms. During the Romantic era, painters strove to liberate themselves from the purely decorative wishes of their paymasters: as for writers and composers, it was a time of increasing autonomy, with both freedom and insecurity the inevitable corollaries. The European political situation, dominated for the best part of three decades by war, ironically forced British artists to seek inspiration closer to home. They thus developed distinctively British modes of painting, particularly of landscapes, and were to some extent freed from conventional, classical models derived from continental sources. The experiences of three major British artists may serve to illustrate the contrasts, tensions and issues of the Romantic era: William Turner (1775–1851), John Constable (1776–1837) and Samuel Palmer (1805–1881).

Turner has been called 'the greatest landscape artist of England and one of the greatest in the world' (from Raymond Lister *British Romantic Painting*, 1989). In many ways, he was typically Romantic in his contradictions – particularly in the tension between his intensely private, complex self and his ambitious search, significantly fulfilled in his own lifetime, for fame and fortune. The contradictions are apparent too in the art he produced: a painter of landscapes intent on capturing reality in paint, he was nevertheless largely uninterested in the substance or detail of landscape. As noted by the art historian David Blayney Brown in

Romanticism (2001):

> … for Turner, reproducing through paint the energy and flux of natural forces, whether of waves or clouds or of the sparkle of light, was central to the dramatic character of his landscape art. It was through this sense of drama that he sought to provide the kind of new direction for landscape …, and paint was the language in which it must be acted.

Energy, power, light: these are the key aspects of Turner's work, and they are definitively Romantic notions. Turner's contemporary, William Hazlitt (1778–1830), a tireless and often sharply perceptive commentator on things Romantic, suggested that his paintings were 'pictures of nothing, and very like', and there may well be something in this. Certainly, Turner's work verges on the abstract, and it is here that his appeal is perhaps most modern. His truthfulness in painting nature derives not so much from any photographic rendering, faithful in every detail, but rather in expressing the emotional power of natural forces as experienced by a susceptible human being. In his comments on his own painting 'Snow Storm – Steam-Boat off a Harbour's Mouth …' (1842), Turner wrote:

> I did not paint it to be understood, but I wished to show what such a scene was like; I got the sailors to lash me to the mast to observe it [the storm]; I was lashed for four hours, and I did not expect to escape, but I felt bound to record it if I did.

In this self-dramatising way, Turner added to the gathering Romantic notion – almost a myth – of the artist as wilfully suffering, to the point of self-sacrifice, for the sake of art.

John Constable was an altogether quieter sort of Romantic artist – although many would wonder whether it is he rather than Turner who could claim to be England's greatest landscape painter. His favoured location, as if to underline his quieter appeal, was his birthplace and the countryside around: Dedham Vale and the Stour Valley in deepest rural Suffolk, still preserved today as 'Constable Country'. When visiting the favoured Romantic landscape of the Lake District in 1806, he found that 'the solitude of the mountains oppressed his spirits', and yearned to return to more familiar surroundings. Although he lived most of his adult life in London, Constable returned constantly to his memories of Suffolk as the source of his paintings: as a vivid illustration of Wordsworth's idea that good art should represent 'emotion recollected in tranquillity'. Constable himself acknowledged this, writing in 1821: 'I associate my careless boyhood with all that lies on the banks of the Stour; those scenes made me a painter, and I am grateful.'

Nevertheless – or perhaps precisely because of the recollection of innocence in viewing landscape – there is plenty of subtle emotional power in Constable's paintings. This is particularly evident in his oil sketches, intended as the basis for later, grander finished works, but now celebrated in their own right. Emotion is in fact central to Constable's idea of art, as he observed in a letter in 1821: 'painting is with me but another word for feeling'.

Even William Blake, never one to shy away from criticising other artists, acknowledged the inspired quality of Constable's art. In the only recorded conversation between the two men, Blake, commenting on a sketch of fir trees on Hampstead Heath in one of Constable's sketchbooks, exclaimed, 'Why, this is not drawing but inspiration!', to which the rather more prosaic – and perhaps disingenuous – Constable replied, 'I never knew it before; I meant it for drawing.' The art historian Hugh Honour makes a provocative distinction between Turner and Constable when he comments that

> … whereas Constable's landscapes seem to reflect both the anguish and the exaltation of intense private prayer, Turner's are more like the product of passionate physical intercourse with his medium, often akin to lovemaking and sometimes to rape.
>
> (from *Romanticism*, 1991)

It is possible to acknowledge both artists as characteristically and intensely Romantic, but representing different aspects of the phenomenon, illustrating the developing breadth of Romantic art and as such reflecting, and contextualising, similar developments in literature.

Whereas both Turner and Constable found significant popular and critical success in their own lifetimes, Samuel Palmer certainly did not – and neither was he anywhere near as prolific. Palmer's reputation is largely posthumous, and for many he represents a mere footnote to artistic history: an idiosyncratic, other-worldly painter, initially attracted to Blake's ideals, but who quickly lost his inspiration and faded into anonymity. There may of course be a grain of truth in this evaluation, but it is far from the whole story. In the 1820s, Palmer and several colleagues, inspired by facets of Blake's work – particularly his miniature woodcuts illustrating Thornton's 'Virgil', intimate and mystically suggestive – retreated from London to the Kentish village of Shoreham. There they established themselves as the 'Ancients', and, for a few years, Palmer produced pictures of breathtaking, visionary beauty. In these works there may be seen a mature, Romantic synthesis between the subjective, religiously inspired imagination, and the beauty of the Shoreham landscape. They reflect the profoundly Platonic idea – a favourite theme of many Romantics, including Blake and Coleridge – that this world is a symbolic pointer to a far greater truth.

Some years before Palmer came to Shoreham, Blake had written that, 'Man has no body distinct from his soul; for that called body is a portion of soul discerned by the five senses, the chief inlets of soul in this age', giving younger Romantics like Palmer a context and sense of direction within which to experiment and develop. Palmer himself wrote in 1828:

> I doubt not but that there must be the study of this creation, as well as art and vision; tho' I cannot think it other than the veil of heaven, through which her divine features are dimly smiling; the setting of the table before the feast; the symphony [overture in modern terminology] before the tune; the prologue of the drama; the dream of antepast and proscenium of eternity.

In a letter of the same year to his fellow artist, John Linnell, Palmer elaborated further, leaving no doubt that nature provides only a platform – albeit a beautiful, appealing one – from which inspired art may spring:

> Everywhere curious, articulate, perfect … Nature does yet leave a space for the soul to climb above her steepest summits: as, in her own dominion she swells from the herring to leviathan; from the hodmandod [a snail] to the elephant, so divine Art piles mountains on her hills, and continents upon those mountains.

Elsewhere, in his 1824–1825 sketchbook, Palmer used poetry to evoke the kind of atmosphere and setting he found most fitting for his particular vision of nature – twilight – with a sense of magic and mystery:

> Methinks the lingering, dying ray
> Of twilight time, doth seem more fair
> And lights the soul up more than day,
> When wide-spread sultry sunshines are

Interestingly, although they produced dramatically different art, the three roughly contemporaneous artists featured here could all lay claim to be central to the development of Romanticism – if, indeed, they were aware of such a development at the time. All three shared a sense of art as an all-enveloping vocation, with the power to transcend everyday notions of reality both for the artists concerned and for their audiences. There occurred a growing sense of the artist as pioneering explorer. In this, pictorial art and literature, especially poetry, were very closely allied.

Romantic attitudes to nature

Inevitably, given the frequent subject matter of the paintings in question, substantial parts of the previous section have touched upon Romantic conceptions of and attitudes towards nature. In any appraisal of Romanticism, it would be hard to avoid the subject. It may well be that in modern ideas on nature, including the ecological preoccupations of our day, there is the greatest and most lasting debt to Romanticism. But, as with so much else, the matter is far from simple: the various poets, composers, artists and commentators discussed so far in this book should already show this clearly enough. The term 'nature' itself is problematic, especially if juxtaposed with ideas about 'culture' – which in a sense is what Romanticism is all about. As Terry Eagleton observed by way of introduction to his book *The Idea of Culture* (2000):

> 'Culture' is said to be one of the two or three most complex words in the English language, and the term which is sometimes considered to be its opposite – nature – is commonly awarded the accolade of being the most complex of all.

As ever, Blake provides a convenient and illuminating touchstone in this context, if only because his views were so definite and so vehemently expressed. In the previously cited conversation between Blake and Constable (page 47), focusing on the nature of the painter's inspiration, there is a strong suggestion of Blake's views on nature and the artistic process: that its accurate representation in art, taken as an end in itself, is vastly inferior to inspiration. Blake himself hardly ever copied nature directly in his art, and neither did he seek to evoke natural surroundings in his poetry. Yet he was a keen observer of the world around him, using aspects of nature as a kind of symbolic language to signify human and spiritual values. His reactions to Constable's drawing suggest this, as do his comments on Wordsworth's preoccupation with nature. Wordsworth, in many respects the poetic equivalent to Constable in his appreciation and love of nature, had written, by way of introduction to Volume 1 of his *Poems*, that 'the powers requisite for the production of poetry are, first, those of observation and description … secondly, sensibility'. Blake responded indignantly, using upper case for emphasis, that 'One Power alone makes a Poet: Imagination, The Divine Vision.' Later in the same volume, Wordsworth, referring to his own childhood, wrote somewhat wistfully:

> And I could wish my days to be
> Bound each to each by natural piety.

Upon which Blake commented, in characteristically bold handwriting in the margins: 'There is no such Thing as Natural Piety because The Natural Man is at Enmity with God.' Some few pages further on, Wordsworth's lines recalling the

> Influence of natural objects
> In calling forth and strengthening the imagination
> In boyhood and early youth

attracted further condemnation from Blake, who commented that 'Natural Objects always did and now do weaken, deaden and obliterate Imagination in Me. Wordsworth must know that what he Writes Valuable is Not to be found in Nature.'

As with so many of Blake's pronouncements on the views of others, especially when concerned with his pet themes of imagination and inspiration, it is important to read these remarks carefully. The context here, as in the reported conversation with Constable, is that of a dialogue, and Blake often deliberately adopted an adversarial position for the sake of argument: as he himself wrote, 'Opposition is true friendship.' Apparently Blake, a Londoner first and foremost, delighted in natural surroundings from the time of his boyhood, and there is a vivid if rather stylised quality to his natural **imagery** in both verse and illustrations. Nevertheless, the developing dialogue is significant, with one viewpoint venerating nature as a quasi-mystical force and the other finding the source of inspiration not in the outside world but in the human mind itself. The underlying tension here informed the development of Romanticism and subsequent views of humanity and the world, and is still very much in evidence in the modern world.

Wordsworth, the object of Blake's indignant criticism, in many ways embodied the alternative Romantic view, to the point of worshipping Nature – ascribing upper case 'N' importance to the word itself. Wordsworth's own childhood, documented exhaustively in his long (and unfinished) autobiographical poem *The Prelude*, provided him with the raw material of the natural landscape of the English Lake District, which would inform his life's work. The evidence for this can be found throughout his verse, and it is small wonder that he has been called a pantheist – one who believes that God is alive in all living things, which are therefore worthy of religious worship.

As with Blake, however, the crux of the matter lies in the relationship between the world outside – in this instance, the natural world of hills, valleys, rivers and woods – and the mind of the artist. Although there may be something of a gulf between the two poets in this context, and between others sharing similar views in varying degrees, the focus on this crucial relationship was sharp in both cases. It may well be that, in the end, the distinction between views which at first sight seem distinctly oppositional, is one of degree rather than of kind. In 'Lines Written in Early Spring', for instance, Wordsworth wrote:

I heard a thousand blended notes,
While in a grove I sate reclined,
In that sweet mood when pleasant thoughts
Bring sad thoughts to the mind.

To her fair works did Nature link
The human soul that through me ran;
And much it grieved my heart to think
What man has made of man.

Implied here is a balanced relationship between the human sensibility – man – and the context of natural surroundings. The balance was certainly different from that found in Blake – it is far more weighted in favour of the benign forces of nature – but is the essence of this meditative poem. In the centrally important poem 'Lines Written a Few Miles above Tintern Abbey' (1798), Wordsworth returns to and develops the theme, maintaining (in a melancholy frame of mind, fearful of losing inspiration):

… Therefore am I still
A lover of the meadows and the woods,
And mountains; and of all that we behold
From this green earth; of all the mighty world
Of eye, and ear, – both what they half create,
And what perceive; well pleased to recognise
In nature and the language of the sense,
The anchor of my purest thoughts, the nurse,
The guide, the guardian of my heart, and soul
Of all my moral being.

The art critic and biographer of Wordsworth, Herbert Read, has written tellingly of this fundamental aspect of Wordsworth's thought:

The individual mind … is exquisitely fitted to the external world and no less exquisitely the external world is fitted to the mind. But it is a marriage of essences, and indeed the whole of Wordsworth's conception of Man and Nature can be conceived under such an analogy. The mind with him is always the creative masculine principle; Nature is always the feminine or reproductive principle.

(from *Wordsworth*, 1953)

In this at least there is a striking similarity between Wordsworth and Blake, and a feminist critique of the Romantic views on nature will be considered below. Read went on to broaden the scope of his analysis to perceive certain characteristically Romantic views of nature, noting first in *Wordsworth*:

> ... the absence of sentimentality in his attitude towards Nature. ... For Wordsworth ... Nature had her own life, which was independent of ours, though a part of the same Godhead. Man and Nature, Mind and the external world, are geared together and in unison complete the motive principle of the universe. They act and react upon each other, 'so as to produce an infinite complexity of pain and pleasure'. The exquisite functioning of this interlocked universe of Mind and Nature is for Wordsworth the highest theme of poetry; in poetry the process actually receives its final consummation.

Through all this, Read was concerned to distinguish between the philosophical seriousness of Wordsworth's position and the merely descriptive nature poetry which is often taken to be 'romantic' (note the lower case 'r' here): this kind of romantic approach 'projects into Nature his own feelings and sentiments. The poet's joy or melancholy is transferred to natural objects, or rather, a selection is made of natural objects in which a sympathetic analogy can be traced, and these objects are endowed with the appropriate mood.'

Clear from Read's exposition is a sense of the importance of both art and nature in the developing Romantic world view. The countryside had indeed been a feature of both poetry and pictorial art throughout the 18th century, but generally as a rather sentimentalised backdrop; with the Romantics it began to hold centre stage. As David Punter puts it:

> ... the dimension of the mythic creeps in with a writer like Wordsworth, with his implicit claim that the countryside is the repository of eternal verities, truths of the imagination which will survive in unchanged form when the urbanisation of Britain has receded like a muddy tide. ... What Wordsworth brings to the ironic tradition [of the 18th century] in *Lyrical Ballads* (1798), *The Prelude* (1805) and elsewhere is an undeviating seriousness. The writer or artist who remains in the city is not merely foolish but immoral; he is cutting himself off from all that is best in humanity, and thus the quality of his work is bound to suffer.
>
> (from *The Romantic Age in Britain*, ed. Boris Ford, 1992)

The idea of the natural as somehow purer, more wholesome, which informs so much of the modern tourist industry – not to mention the basis of much advertising for foods, cosmetics and other products – derives from such a Romantic position.

Feminist readings of Romantic attitudes to nature

In more recent times, the critical context for Romanticism has been significantly enhanced by feminist appraisals of the period and its artistic creations. Not surprisingly, a good deal of this critical examination has focused on Romantic conceptions of nature, as has already been noted. If nature is seen as fundamentally submissive – fertile, inspiring but ultimately feminine and malleable – and the act of creation as powerfully manipulative in masculine terms, then there is clearly a tension at the heart of Romanticism. Aidan Day, in his close critical reading of sections of Wordsworth's *The Prelude* (1805 version) illuminates a feminist critique of the interplay between nature and the imagination, concluding that:

> Nature thus can offer a 'resemblance' of the 'glorious faculty' of higher minds. Nature can herself intimate something beyond herself: the soul, the imagination of the whole. The 'herself' is important here. Nature is characterised as feminine. But the feminine is here associated with something that is not in itself of ultimate importance. Feminine nature simply directs towards the reality of ultimate importance which lies beyond nature herself. What is really of importance … is the male speaker's mind, his imagination, which participates in and apprehends the ultimate mind, imagination or 'Deity'. The **sublime** moment is peculiarly male. Nature and the feminine can help facilitate this moment of sublime apprehension, but that is as far as it goes.
>
> (from *Romanticism*,1996)

Significantly, feminist readings have uncovered and developed a radically different view of nature as presented by Dorothy Wordsworth – for so long regarded simply as a ready mentor and facilitator for the great poetry of her brother William. Feminist critics such as Margaret Homans and Meena Alexander have demonstrated that for Dorothy Wordsworth nature is allowed to live and breathe without the intervening – and perhaps polluting – force of the (invariably male) ego in the way. There is perhaps a suggestion of a more ecological view of, and respect for, nature here – striking in the light of modern concerns. Alexander, for example, notes that 'the visible world … in Dorothy's finest writings … gathers powers and luminosity precisely to the extent to which it is shorn of the overt hold of the self' (Alexander, 1989, quoted in Aidan Day *Romanticism*, 1996).

The modern film *Pandemonium* (2001) rather sensationally traces the development of the relationship between the Wordsworths and Coleridge, attempting to show vividly that true inspiration belonged with Dorothy and Coleridge – both of whom suffered from debilitating opium addictions, which in Dorothy's case, according to this interpretation, led to her insanity and subsequent incarceration by her brother. The imagery of this film leaves no doubt that attitudes towards nature lie at the very heart of Romanticism, and of these eventually dislocated personal relationships in particular.

Assignments

1 Making use of the Time line on pages 6–7 and any other available resources, write an introductory handbook entitled 'The Student's Guide to Romanticism' (or another title of your choice). The target readership here is future students of Romanticism. It may be appropriate to work collaboratively, with specific tasks and themes such as:
   • historical and contemporary manifestations of Romanticism
   • artistic presentations of Romanticism in broad terms
   • selected quotations with your own annotations
   • social and political contexts
   • emphasis on audience – the consumer
   • biographical sketches of the key figures in the development of Romanticism.

2 Carefully selecting your materials, build up a collection of quotations to accompany chosen illustrations – from both historical and contemporary Romantic sources – to present a vivid 'flavour' of what Romanticism actually means to you in terms of its manifestations. ICT, the scanner and the photocopier could be useful here, as well as traditional cutting and pasting. Such material may be most effectively presented as a collage, which you could talk through and explain orally to an audience. The assignment may be extended to include more diverse examples of the Romantic, such as clips from films, musical extracts and a range of artefacts.

3 In the light of your reading and thinking about Romantic attitudes to the countryside and to nature in general, research tourist brochures and travel literature – perhaps particularly those which focus on the burgeoning 'heritage industry' – to ascertain just how far they rely on Romantic approaches. This study could be extended to encompass aspects of environmental and ecological presentations throughout the media.

2 | Approaching the texts

- Which elements might make a literary text 'Romantic'?

- Which elements might make a Romantic text literary?

- How might the various areas looked at in Part 1 actually be represented in Romantic texts?

- What sort of similarities and contrasts may be shown by the range of Romantic writers under consideration?

Part 2: Approaching the texts analyses how some of the Romantic preoccupations and broad characteristics examined in Part 1 manifest themselves in literary (in other words, imaginative and fictional) texts. A range of different aspects of Romanticism will be considered, each related to specific texts and frequently building on textual exploration already undertaken in Part 1. Reference will be made also to the texts and extracts included in Part 3. There are more questions posed, as well as further tasks and imaginative assignments to stimulate thought, as the background understanding and knowledge of Romanticism gained from Part 1 is further applied.

Textual characteristics of Romanticism

The first question posed above – which elements might make a literary text 'Romantic' – is an important one, not least because of the difficulties and ambiguities involved in defining Romanticism in the first place. Two secondary questions, following on from that fundamental issue, may help to clarify and amplify possible meaning:

- How important is the term 'Romantic' in understanding the nature of a particular text?

- How may the application of the label 'Romantic' either enhance or limit textual understanding and appreciation?

These suggested questions imply that the use of the term 'Romantic' may help in reaching a properly contextualised understanding of a text, but may also be a hindrance if it over-defines and possibly closes down what should be an open, imaginative response. As with broad defining characteristics of Romanticism as a whole, a careful approach is needed: sweeping generalisations and definitions applied to real actions carried out by real people – including diverse artistic endeavours – can be misleading. Reality rarely conforms to any stereotype. However, with this important stipulation in mind, it may be helpful at this stage to clarify what tentatively defined qualities may be seen in a Romantic text. No text is likely to display all of the characteristics noted below, and some may be mutually exclusive; nevertheless, the list should be helpful as a starting point:

- Texts generally showed signs of deep emotional impact. In lyrical poetry this was often through the feelings of the poet, or an adopted persona; in longer poems, especially narrative verse, and in novels there was likely to be exploration of the emotional lives of several characters.

- Related to this point, there was a development of the use of imagery and **symbolism** to convey often subtle emotional significance. This could be in terms of either the internal world of the imagination, or of external reality.

- Consequently, there was a conscious search for appropriately imaginative settings for texts, often using familiar aspects of nature, and sometimes more deliberately exotic settings.

- Qualities such as innocence and wonder, child-like sensibilities, extremes of feeling verging on insanity, imaginative excess were frequently characteristic of Romantic subject matter.

- Individuality was often emphasised, sometimes in terms of glorious defiance of conventional standards and codes, sometimes in less glorious explorations of alienation and distinctly anti-social, destructive urges.

- Spiritual, ethical, psychological and political explorations, usually questioning established views, became the frequent subject matter of Romantic texts – whether through direct statement, or through more tentative exploration.

The list could be extended, to make ever more subtle suggestions of commonly found Romantic textual tendencies, but this list should be sufficient to give a sense of focus for further study, informing more detailed examination. In many respects, the areas mentioned have arisen from the contextual explorations already undertaken in Part 1. In some areas especially – the emphasis on innocence, for example, or the sense of apt settings in nature – there has already been significant textual as well as contextual exploration. This is no accident, and is meant to illustrate the close unity and inextricable inter-relationship between context and text, the one feeding off and contributing to the other. The same sense of cross-fertilisation should inform your approach to the reading of Romantic texts.

▶ In the light of the range of textual characteristics found in Romantic texts listed above, explore again some of the Romantic texts you have encountered. These may be the various extracts cited in Part 1: Approaching Romanticism, or some of the examples from Part 3: Texts and extracts, or your own broader explorations. The idea is to relate the possible characteristics to the texts you have chosen, in a spirit of critical questioning and open discussion.

Romantic language

Writing, clearly the most durable form of language, was central to Romanticism. As has already been seen in various examples, exponents of other art forms, such as artists and musicians, turned also to writing to explain their – often distinctly Romantic – intentions. As David Punter puts it:

> … the years 1785–1851 are most importantly recorded in writing. … We are dealing here with a period when the expansion of education was largely focused on issues of literacy, and the word is easily the most accessible form of communication. … we may hypothesise that it is the written word that most resonantly encapsulates national aspiration and national discord, for the simple reason that we are here dealing with language, and language is the substance of national identity.
>
> (from *The Romantic Age in Britain,* ed. Boris Ford, 1992)

Romantic language developed in this context, but, as ever, the relationship between text – the examples of language – and context was not a simple one. Whereas standards of literacy increased, as suggested, opening up new readership potential, many Romantics also saw themselves as cultivating esoteric – deliberately 'difficult' – language precisely to counter what could be seen as the threat of debasement of the written word through overuse.

For many of the Romantics it was the language of poetry that epitomised the language of intense feeling and creative imagination. It is perhaps small wonder that today many people could, if pressed, name the 'big six' English Romantic poets – Blake, Wordsworth, Coleridge, Shelley, Byron and Keats – as somehow representing the high point of Romanticism, with various relatively minor poets – Clare, Scott and Burns, for example – swimming in their wake. Finding a definition for poetry is notoriously difficult, and it may well be that in its elusive nature it has something particularly in common with Romanticism itself.

However, most poets and critics would agree that any defining characteristics for poetry would have to include its self-conscious use of language for effect, including rhythmic and sound qualities, its expression of intensity of feeling, and its concision. All of these elements – and many more, for that matter – could be conveniently summarised in the phrase 'language working hard'. And that is precisely how the Romantics liked their language to work, making poetry a kind of distillation of the intentions and effects of the Romantic world view.

The idea of language working hard also implies high seriousness, and here again there is something appropriate to Romanticism – and that despite, or perhaps because of, the deliberately playful nature of so much poetic language. In a sense this reflects again the distinction between 'childish', as inconsequential and facile, and child-like, as suggesting the seriousness of a child at play and the sense of wonder arising from innocence: a distinction, perhaps, central to Romanticism.

It is of course important to appreciate that poetry was not the only language expressing the Romantic sense of the world. There were huge developments in the language of prose as well, examples of which are included in this book, in terms of both fiction and non-fiction. Yet time and time again it is poetry which is most suggestive of Romanticism.

Hugh Honour makes the point that the qualities of poetry make it more than simply the most appropriate mode of written expression; something about the nature of poetry seems to embody the spirit of Romanticism itself: 'The Romantics were more deeply concerned with qualities than rules, with integrity of feeling than with rectitude of judgement – with poetry than with prosody.' (from *Romanticism,* 1991). Words expressing this emphasis, such as 'sensibility' and 'genius', gained enormous currency to testify to the development of the Romantic spirit, and their implications were taken up enthusiastically by a range of poets writing across a variety of poetic genres. Ballads, lyrical poems, poems for children, poetry celebrating nature, and verse of psychological reflection were in the ascendant, and all of these are represented in Part 3 of this book.

▶ Keeping in mind the reflections on the nature of poetry and Romanticism above, look carefully at the selection of Romantic verse included in Part 3: Texts and extracts. Blake, Wordsworth, Coleridge, Shelley, Byron, Clare, More and Keats are all quintessentially Romantic, yet their differences are clear. Try to judge just how far their poems included here have Romantic qualities in common, and in what respects they differ from each other.

The search for Romantic settings

In many ways the world was opened up to Western European eyes by the spirit of Romanticism – both far and wide in sometimes hitherto unexplored areas, and in seeing more immediate surroundings with a new sense of wonder. The former urge may be seen clearly in the 'discovery' of relatively isolated, thinly populated areas of Britain such as the Lake District, Snowdonia, and the Highlands of Scotland. These regions were destined to become tourist magnets, designated 'areas of outstanding natural beauty' in no small part because of their attraction to the early Romantics. Further afield, the dramatic scenery of the Alps became a favourite venue for artists and writers, and for upper-class tourists who had previously limited themselves to the great European cities and centres of culture. The urge to find beauty and wonder close to home, came to be represented in artists such as Constable, focusing on the Suffolk of his boyhood, and Palmer in Shoreham, Kent. It also came to be represented in poets such as John Clare, who was deeply attached to his native Northamptonshire, and whose first volume of verse was entitled, aptly enough, *Poems Descriptive of Rural Life and Scenery* (1820).

In the sense that the Romantics were concerned with exploring new terrain in terms of human feelings and imaginative qualities, their search for appropriate settings in nature and in private worlds of fantasy was deeply significant. For it is the settings which should, if effective, awaken the reader or audience to a heightened awareness of the message. As David Punter observes '… we can see in it [Romantic experience] a constant search for settings adequate as models and correlatives for the human mind' (from *The Romantic Age in Britain,* ed. Boris Ford, 1992). The German Romantic philosopher Johann Fichte (1762–1814) went so far as to suggest that we invent or create the world as we perceive it, and that it has no real existence independent of these perceptions; this is an extreme subjectivist position, typifying what was becoming known as German philosophical idealism. Yet it has a profound relevance for the Romantic search for settings. In the relationship between the subjective (the mind, or, more Romantically, the imagination) and the objective (the world) lies the true significance of the setting. It should both occasion the poetic, or creative, urge, and in some sense embody it.

Much of this mode of feeling has its roots in that favourite Romantic concept: the sublime, and in particular Edmund Burke's influential study *A Philosophical Enquiry into the Origin of Our Ideas of the Sublime and Beautiful* (1757). The focus here was on the human reaction to an overwhelming experience that transcends everyday normality. It is hardly surprising that Burke's words had such a great impact, as they succinctly state what so much Romantic art was striving for in finding the appropriate setting:

> Whilst we contemplate so vast an object, under the arm, as it were, of almighty power, and invested on every side with omnipresence, we shrink into the minuteness of our own nature, and are, in a manner, annihilated before him.

▶ With particular reference to Wordsworth's important meditative poem 'Lines Written a Few Miles above Tintern Abbey, on revisiting the banks of the Wye during a tour' (1798), and in the light of the points discussed above, examine and evaluate the significance of setting in the poem. Look closely at the attitude the poet takes towards his chosen setting, and how his view may change and modulate through the course of the poem. As an extension of this task, you could go on to compare the poet's outlook here to other poems by Wordsworth, and to poetic works by other Romantics such as Coleridge and Clare.

Developing critical insights

One of the peculiarities of the Romantic transformation of culture and the arts – for transformation it turned out to be – was its sense of its own significance. Artists started taking themselves seriously, as has already been amply evidenced in this book. The signs of this new seriousness can be discerned in the works of art themselves (perhaps especially in poetry), in the explanatory writings of the artists responsible, and in the insights of critics. It was the last category which was particularly noteworthy. Most of the important Romantic poets played their part in the development of the appropriate critical climate for their own and others' work to take root and thrive, especially if they lived long enough to command the respect and even attain the wisdom that old age sometimes brings. Blake's comments about the nature of poetry and the imagination have already been fairly extensively cited, and his letter to the rather more literal minded, sceptical Reverend Trusler, which states his position clearly, is included in Part 3 (page 75). Further examples of this kind of insight might include the philosopher and critic Novalis, who observed in 1798 that 'poetry is the genuine absolute Reality. That is the kernel of my philosophy. The more poetic, the truer.' They might include Wordsworth, writing in the same year, when he maintained in the Preface to the *Lyrical Ballads* that 'poetry is the first and last of all knowledge – it is as immortal as the heart of man'. There is a distinct sense here of the role of the arts not merely to entertain, far less to divert, but rather to transform the world for the better. In essence, during the Romantic epoch, the arts became the signifiers of human possibility.

A vitally important, and much discussed, example of poets stating their purpose beyond the verse itself came with the Preface to the 1798 Edition of *Lyrical Ballads,* jointly written by Coleridge and Wordsworth (although now largely ascribed to the latter), added to the collection in 1800, and revised in 1802. (An extract is included in Part 3, page 83.) The key ideas in this Preface are to do with the subject matter of the ensuing poems, the language through which they are expressed, and the emotional and mental conditions which gave rise to them in the first place.

In the context of the late 18th century, with Britain embroiled in counter-revolutionary warfare at home and abroad, the controversially democratic intentions are clear:

The principal object, then, proposed in these Poems, was to choose

incidents and situations from common life, and to relate or describe
them throughout, as far as was possible, in a selection of language
really used by men …

This may not sound particularly radical, but the political context made it so. The
idea of rooting poetry in the activities and lives of ordinary men and women was
perceived at the time as distinctly – and, depending on the point of view,
dangerously – democratic.

In terms of the actual construction of the poems, there was more to say: a
realisation that the simple relating of rural incidents through plain English would
hardly constitute poetry, especially not the great poetry that Wordsworth and
Coleridge seriously intended. The previous quotation continues '… and, at the
same time, to throw over them a certain colouring of imagination, whereby
ordinary things should be presented to the mind in an unusual aspect …'. This
insistence on the power of the imagination to shape experiences was of course a
profoundly Romantic notion. The crux of the Preface lies in the balance, or tension,
between the initial impressions and attendant emotions of the poet, and the self-
conscious, intellectually-based craft in fashioning a finished work of art:

For all good poetry is the spontaneous overflow of powerful feelings:
and though this be true, Poems to which any value can be attached
were never produced on any variety of subjects but by a man who,
being possessed of more than usual organic sensibility, had also
thought long and deeply.

Critics have been divided as to the impact and originality of this Preface, and indeed
as to the significance of the *Lyrical Ballads* collection as a whole. There has been a
distinct tendency to see Wordsworth as the senior partner in the enterprise, and
certainly he provided the majority of the poems and apparently wrote most of the
Preface. Marilyn Butler, in *Romantics, Rebels and Reactionaries* (1981) initiates a
helpful discussion on the various critical appraisals, focusing on Wordsworth,
having nailed her own colours to the mast with her opening statement: 'We should
dismiss at the outset the belief, still widely held, that Wordsworth's contributions to
the *Lyrical Ballads* of 1798 represent an altogether new kind of poetry.'

Earlier commentators have often seen rather more originality in the
fundamental ethos of the collection and its Preface. The eminent Victorian man of
letters, Matthew Arnold, celebrated in exalted prose the new naturalness professed
by Wordsworth:

Nature herself seems, I say, to take the pen out of his hand, and to
write for him with her own bare, sheer, penetrating power. This arises

from two causes; from the profound sincereness with which Wordsworth feels his subject, and also from the profoundly sincere and natural character of his subject itself. He can and will treat such a subject with nothing but the most plain, first-hand, almost austere naturalness. His expression may often be called bald ...; but it is bald as the bare mountain tops are bald, with a baldness which is full of grandeur.

(from Essays and Criticism, 1879)

This sort of appraisal set the tone for over a century of acclaim, still reflected in Helen Derbishire's study *The Poet Wordsworth* (1950): 'Wordsworth's was a revolt of a nature and importance which perhaps no literary revolt had before. It was a revolt against literature, or the literary element in poetry, an assertion of the supreme value of life at all costs in poetry.' Whichever critical position is taken, it should be abundantly clear that, in approaching Romantic texts, the *Lyrical Ballads* and their Preface cannot be ignored.

▶ Keeping in mind the various points made about the nature of poetry by Wordsworth and by his critics, look carefully at the poems included in *Lyrical Ballads,* both those included in Part 3: Texts and extracts and those in other sources. Through close critical reading, try to decide which elements of the Preface are actually fulfilled in the poems themselves. Is a balance between natural spontaneity and the craft of making a poem successfully achieved?

The Romantic as sage: Coleridge

The relationship between Wordsworth and Coleridge has been the focus of fascinated enquiry from their own time to ours, and has undergone frequent revisions of emphasis and interpretation. There are, effectively, two extreme positions: on the one hand, it is possible to see Wordsworth as a rock of practical stability, offering to protect and guide the wayward and often feckless Coleridge, even when ungratefully spurned; on the other hand, Coleridge may be seen as the personification of the Romantic gifted genius, jealously thwarted by the more prosaic presence of Wordsworth. The modern film *Pandemonium* (2001) certainly develops the latter of these positions, accusing Wordsworth of deliberately setting out to destroy the creative talents of both Coleridge and his own sister Dorothy – talents far greater than his own – for a variety of selfish, and even politically reactionary, motives. Over the two centuries since their own time, however, most critics have presented positions somewhere between the two poles outlined. What is significant, it seems, is the continuing fascination with the two poets' lives as context for their works.

Coleridge became as famous for his thoughts on the nature of poetry as for his poetry itself. Indeed virtually all of his well-known verse – including 'The Rime of the Ancient Mariner' and 'Kubla Khan' – was written in the early part of his life, when, perhaps decisively, his relationship with Wordsworth was at its most harmonious and productive. In his middle and later years, fighting an increasingly losing battle against ill-health, disappointment in love, and opium addiction, Coleridge wrote comparatively little poetry, but he energetically read, wrote and lectured about Romantic conceptions of culture. He became known, especially to the younger generation of Romantics, as the 'Sage of Highgate' after the North London suburb, then a village, where he lived and where the house in which he lodged (and the shop from where he bought his opium) may still be seen. His wide-ranging lectures were eventually enthusiastically attended, and his major work, reflecting on the role of the creative artist in context, *Biographia Literaria,* has become a central text of the Romantic era. A couple of quotations from this 'literary biography' should serve to account for its reputation, and give a flavour of the prose:

> The poet, described in ideal perfection, brings the whole soul of man into activity, with the subordination of its faculties to each other, according to their relative worth and dignity. ... Finally, GOOD SENSE is the BODY of the poetic genius, FANCY its DRAPERY, MOTION its LIFE, and IMAGINATION the SOUL that is everywhere, and in each; and forms all into one graceful and intelligent whole.
>
> (Vol II, Ch 14)

A little further on, elaborating on the supreme quality of the imagination, the emphasis is on its central function for Romanticism:

> The IMAGINATION then, I consider either as primary or secondary. The primary IMAGINATION I hold to be the living Power and prime Agent of all human Perception, and as a repetition in the finite mind of the eternal act of creation in the infinite I AM. The secondary Imagination I consider as an echo of the former, co-existing with the conscious will, yet still as identical with the primary in the kind of its agency, and differing only in degree, and in the mode of its operation.
>
> (Vol II, Ch 22)

In many ways Coleridge personified the contradictions and tensions of the age. Supremely gifted and accomplished, he nevertheless left many of his projects – in personal as well as artistic terms – unfinished. Powerfully innovative, even revolutionary, he was at the same time drawn to conventional values of the past, and eventually became one of the inspirers of conservative thought. Possessed of a startlingly original mind, he has been accused of plagiarism from contemporary German philosophers, perhaps with some justification. However, his seminal importance as thinker, despite or even because of his contradictions, has been generally acknowledged. As John Beer maintains, 'If there was a particular writer to whom most others related it was Samuel Taylor Coleridge; but he was not a leader with a formulated message or programme, rather a man of unusual gifts and intelligence who provoked the thinking of others and who had a decisive influence on a number of young writers during their formative years.' (from *The Romantic Age in Britain,* ed. Boris Ford, 1992). Another critic, Marilyn Butler, has written perceptively about Coleridge as representing, in Britain at least, a profound change in the intellectual climate: 'Coleridge is in fact one of the first representatives in England, and perhaps the most important early representative, of a distinct new type.' (from *Romantics, Rebels and Reactionaries,* 1981). Going on to explore the meaning and significance of this change, which centred on the relatively new-found prestige accorded to a professional artist and thinker, Butler concludes:

> What does emerge earlier [than 1830], most brilliantly with and through Coleridge, is a new recognition of the distinctiveness of the poet as a type. ... Coleridge represents our idea of the artist in its modern variant, and it appears to be necessary that he should be tragic: neurotic, displaced, the Hamlet of our times, an appropriate culture-hero ....

In the light of this observation, it is small wonder that one of the areas that Coleridge did much to pioneer was Shakespeare studies, giving a distinctively Romantic interpretation to much of Shakespeare's work – not least the perennially fascinating figure of Hamlet. Coleridge's own self-written epitaph (1830) is vividly suggestive of the Romantic artist, echoing as it does the ghostly presences of 'The Rime of the Ancient Mariner':

> That he who many a year with toil of breath
> Found death in life, may here find life in death!

▶ Keeping in mind Coleridge's guiding ideas on the nature of the imagination and its centrality to the artist's role, read carefully a selection of his poems, including those featured in Part 3 of this book. If possible, try to discern whether the poet writes himself into his own verse as protagonist: as the tragically possessed Ancient Mariner, for example, condemned to keep re-telling his disturbing tale.

The critical positioning of Romanticism

For the Romantic artist, one direct outcome of the development of the 'distinct new type' represented by Coleridge was an increasingly self-conscious sense of critical significance. Romanticism had set itself up in opposition to the dominant belief in restrained good order, as epitomised by Neo-Classical values, and in so doing could not fail to feel important. Schlegel remarked that artists were to the rest of mankind what human beings were to the rest of creation (in *Critical Writings,* 1800), with more than a hint of the intellectual elitism that would characterise a strand of Romantic thought to this day. As Hugh Honour has noted, with reference to Beethoven, 'Art had ceased to be a trade or profession: it had become a vocation.' (from *Romanticism,* 1991).

The term 'vocation', clearly, suggests a powerful, inspirational calling which cannot be ignored – and in this sense the Romantic spirit of the tortured artist continues to endure. The 'second generation' of British Romantics, Byron, Keats, Shelley and others, inherited from Blake, Coleridge and their fellow-innovators a powerful mission, and high standards to live up to. As Romanticism developed from its late 18th-century beginnings there were, inevitably perhaps, new tensions and contradictions. Never exactly a coherent or unified 'movement', subsequent divergences multiplied as time passed – unsurprising in a way of thinking and feeling that had a strong sense of individualism at its very core.

In a sense too the rebellious, oppositional stance of Romanticism's early days could lead to other problematic issues. What would happen when Romanticism itself became part of the establishment: the dominant – even conventional – mode of feeling? Aggravated tensions, loose fragmentation or some sort of destructive turning in on itself were all distinct possibilities, and all three may be discerned in the history of Romantic ideas and aesthetics during the 19th and 20th centuries. Nevertheless, the spirit of Romanticism survived.

As the sheer volume of human knowledge increased vastly, so did the urge to specialise – most obviously in the divergence of the arts and the sciences. Marilyn Gaull has observed that:

> The gradual fragmentation of human knowledge, the development of various disciplines, with specialised and often opposing methods and values, the collapse of the artificial eighteenth century synthesis of human experience coincided with the Romantic period.
>
> (from *English Romanticism,* 1988)

This was the essential philosophical context of the period, and in a sense the very diversity of ideas and creative forms gave Romanticism a lifeline – a means of celebrating individuality – when the alternative might have been formless disintegration. Clearly the old beliefs and values were increasingly inappropriate for the discoveries, inventions and developments of industrially-based society, and here the spirit of Romanticism played a key role, focusing, characteristically, on the imagination. The arts, newly elevated in importance, according to Gaull:

> … helped to enfranchise the imagination, raising it from a faculty associated with fantasy, falsehood, even insanity to one that could, for artist, philosopher and scientist, overcome the limits of observation and intellect; mediate between the known and the unknown; discern common principles among the variety of natural phenomena that preoccupied scientists, painters and writers alike; formulate responses to change; anticipate consequences; and establish relationships among the increasingly diversified members of the social and intellectual community.

All of these qualities, both positive and negative, may be seen in the personalities and the artistic creations of the central figures in the development of Romanticism. As so often, it may be best here to allow the artists to speak for themselves on the nature of their own art. The radical Shelley, for example, who came nearest of all the major Romantic figures to a position of revolutionary socialism despite his aristocratic background, also had a great deal to say about poetry. There need be no contradiction here: Shelley saw art as a powerful force for revolutionary change, not simply in the political order of the day but in the hearts and souls of humankind. For Shelley:

> Poetry is indeed something divine. It is at once the centre and circumference of knowledge; it is that which comprehends all science, and that to which all science must be referred. It is at the same time the root and blossom of all other systems of thought; it is that from which all spring, and that which adorns all; and that which, if blighted, denies the fruit and the seed, and withholds from the barren world the nourishment and the succession of the scions of the tree of life.
>
> (from 'A Defence of Poetry' in *Complete Works* Vol VII)

Keats, on the other hand, observed wryly, having given two guiding axioms for the judgement of poetry, that '…it is easier to think what poetry should be than to write it – and this leads me on to another axiom. That if poetry comes not as naturally as the leaves to a tree it had better not come at all.' (letter to John Taylor, 1818).

The trouble with short selective quotations like these is that they can over-simplify complex issues and viewpoints. In fact, both Shelley and Keats were aware of the complicated nature of the relationship between the individual and wider society, which is what much of the Romantic philosophical enquiry boils down to. Both saw the need for a total revolution in both individual attitudes and in society, and for an erosion of the barriers between these worlds. For Shelley there was no qualitative difference between spending a large part of his considerable inheritance on writing, printing and distributing revolutionary pamphlets to the Irish peasantry on the one hand, and cultivating his imaginative powers on the other. Keats, who like Shelley died tragically young, developed his key concept of 'negative capability' as a way of enabling individual consciousness to open itself to all experience: 'that is, when man is capable of being in uncertainties, Mysteries, doubts, without any irritable reaching after fact and reason'.

Such openness, for Keats and many Romantics, became the essential precondition for creativity. The alternatives to the kind of synthesis of the individual and society promoted in their different ways by Shelley and Keats were dangerous. Either there would be a losing sight of the individual altogether in the interests of society at large, or, alternatively, a sense that the individual consciousness is the only true reality. John Clare too, in his moving poem 'I Am', included in Part 3 (page 99), saw the limitations of the latter position all too clearly. It is this insistence on creative synthesis between outer and inner worlds which is – potentially at least – the greatest legacy of Romanticism.

▶ Taking poems by Shelley, Keats, and Clare as a touchstone, consider how they develop the crucial relationship between inner and outer worlds. Use poems included in Part 3 of this book, and examples from other sources.

The challenge: Mary Shelley

The challenge to reach some sort of creative synthesis, building on but also questioning Romantic roots, was taken up by Shelley's young wife, Mary. Mary Shelley's pedigree was certainly impressive: she was the daughter of the anarchist philosopher William Godwin and the feminist thinker Mary Wollstonecraft, who died a few days after giving birth (see Part 1, page 33). At the age of 16, Mary started a relationship with the young, but already married, poet Shelley, subsequently eloping abroad and marrying him on his divorce in 1816. Her first and by far her most famous novel, *Frankenstein,* was published anonymously in 1818. The roots of *Frankenstein* lay in the Shelleys' sometimes desperate wanderings through Europe, in the thoughts and activities of her husband and friends like Lord Byron, in the tragic death of her baby daughter, and in her own fertile imagination and reading. The novel itself is challenging in more ways than one, not least in its sustained questioning of the Romantic myth of – generally male – individualism. As Aidan Day observes: '*Frankenstein* pushes the Romantic model of the solitary, creative imagination to its extreme and illustrates its dangerous and destructive propensities.' (from *Romanticism*, 1996).

The actual circumstances of the writing of *Frankenstein* seem as fascinating, and have been the subject of almost as much mythologising, as the novel itself – particularly with the making of comparatively recent films like *Gothic* (1987) and *Rowing with the Wind* (1992). Mary Shelley's own Preface to the later (1831) edition of the novel sheds much light on the creative processes, expressing first her amazement at the feat of her fourteen-years-younger self: 'How I, then a young girl, came to think of, and dilate upon, so very hideous an idea?' There was no lack of immediate inspiration: the company and stimulating conversation of Shelley, Byron and others, in the atmospheric setting of Byron's Swiss villa. During one evening there, Byron suggested to the party that they entertain each other with a competition to find the most frightening ghost story – and this idea clearly meant more than mere recreation to the impressionable Mary Shelley. She later told of her frustration in not finding a suitable theme, until one night, not sleeping:

> My imagination, unbidden, possessed and guided me, gifting the successive images that arose in my mind with a vividness far beyond the usual bounds of reverie. I saw ... the pale student of unhallowed arts kneeling beside the thing he had put together. I saw the hideous phantasm of a man stretched out, and then, on the working of some powerful engine, show signs of life and stir with an uneasy, half vital emotion.
>
> (Preface to *Frankenstein*, 1831)

This was the terrifying image around which the novel was to crystallise; she was then able to announce that she 'had thought of a story', but the extract suggests that her words are tinged with irony, and that the opposite had occurred: the story was in a sense thinking its own medium, its writer. The rest is history.

Frankenstein went on to become one of the central texts of the Romantic era and beyond, as the stimulus for countless film versions right up to our own time. It has been interpreted in a wide range of ways, and some of these readings are considered in Part 4: Critical approaches.

▶ Consider carefully exactly how Mary Shelley's novel *Frankenstein* both challenges key Romantic concepts and ideals, and takes them further as foundations for new, perhaps more subtle and feminist approaches. You could use both the extract included in Part 3 (page 103), and the novel as a whole.

3 | Texts and extracts

The texts and extracts that follow have been chosen to illustrate key themes and points made elsewhere in the book, and to provide material which may be useful when working on the tasks and assignments. The poems and extracts have been arranged in chronological order of the writer's birth date.

Thomas Paine

'On Revolution' from *The Rights of Man* Part 1 (1791)

'Men are born … free' became the political catchphrase of radical Romanticism, and its source is in this extract from Thomas Paine's widely influential text. Paine combined propagandist writing with revolutionary activity, most notably in the American and French Revolutions.

When we survey the wretched condition of man under the monarchical and hereditary systems of government, dragged from his home by one power, or driven by another, and impoverished by taxes more than by enemies, it becomes evident that those systems are bad, and that a general revolution in the principle and construction of governments is necessary.

What is government more than the management of the affairs of a nation? It is not, and from its nature cannot be, the property of any particular man or family, but of the whole community at whose expense it is supported. And though by force or contrivance it has been usurped into an inheritance, the ursurpation cannot alter the right of things. Sovereignty, as a matter of right, appertains to the nation only, and not to any individual; and a nation has at all times an inherent indefeasible right to abolish any form of government it finds inconvenient, and establish such as accords with its interest, disposition and happiness. The romantic and barbarous distinction of men into kings and subjects, though it may suit the condition of courtiers, cannot that of citizens – and is exploded by the principle upon which governments are now founded. Every citizen is a member of the sovereignty, and as such can acknowledge no personal subjection, and his obedience can be only to the laws.

When men think of what government is, they must necessarily suppose it to possess a knowledge of all the objects and matters upon which its authority is to be exercised. In this view of government, the republican system as established by America and France operates to embrace the whole of a nation, and the knowledge necessary to the interest of all the parts is to be found in the centre, which the parts by representation form. But the old governments are on a construction that excludes knowledge as well as happiness – government by monks who know nothing of the world beyond the walls of a convent is as consistent as government by kings.

What were formerly called revolutions were little more than a change of persons or an alteration of local circumstances. They rose and fell like things of course, and had nothing in their existence or their fate that could influence beyond the spot that produced them. But what we now see in the world, from the revolutions of America and France, are a renovation of the natural order of things, a system of principles as universal as truth and the existence of man, and combining moral with political happiness and national prosperity.

I. Men are born and always continue free and equal in respect of their rights. Civil distinctions therefore, can be founded only on public utility.

II. The end of all political associations is the preservation of the natural and imprescriptible rights of man; and these rights are liberty, property, security, and resistance of oppression.

III. The nation is essentially the source of all sovereignty; nor can any individual or any body of men be entitled to any authority which is not expressly derived from it.

In these principles there is nothing to throw a nation into confusion by inflaming ambition. They are calculated to call forth wisdom and abilities, and to exercise them for the public good, and not for the emolument or aggrandisement of particular descriptions of men or families. Monarchical sovereignty – the enemy of mankind and the source of misery – is abolished, and sovereignty itself is restored to its natural and original place: the nation. Were this the case throughout Europe, the cause of wars would be taken away.

Hannah More

From 'The Sorrows of Yamba, or the Negro Woman's Lamentation' (c. 1795)

A famous and successful writer in her time, Hannah More is relatively little known today. She was a member of the women's intellectual group, the Bluestockings, and campaigned throughout her long life for a range of radical causes – in this instance, the movement to abolish slavery.

The Sorrows of Yamba

In St Lucie's distant isle
    Still with Afric's love I burn,
Parted many a thousand mile
    Never, never to return.

Come, kind death, and give me rest!
    Yamba has no friend but thee;
Thou canst ease my throbbing breast,
    Thou canst set the prisoner free.

Down my cheeks the tears are dripping,
    Broken is my heart with grief,
Mangled my poor flesh with whipping;
    Come, kind death, and bring relief!

Born on Afric's golden coast,
    Once I was as blessed as you;
Parents tender I could boast,
    Husband dear, and children too.

Whity man he came from far,
    Sailing o'er the briny flood,
Who, with help of British tar,
    Buys up human flesh and blood.

With the baby at my breast
    (Other two were sleeping by),
In my hut I sat at rest
    With no thought of danger nigh.

From the bush at eventide
    Rushed the fierce man-stealing crew,
Seized the children by my side,
    Seized the wretched Yamba too.

Then for love of filthy gold,
    Straight they bore me to the sea,
Crammed me down a slave-ship's hold
    Where were hundreds stowed like me.

Naked on the platform lying,
   Now we cross the tumbling wave –
Shrieking, sickening, fainting, dying,
   Dead of shame for Britons brave.

At the savage Captain's beck
   Now like brutes they make us prance;
Smack the cat about the deck,
   And in scorn they bid us dance.

I in groaning passed the night,
   And did roll my aching head:
At the break of morning light
   My poor child was cold and dead.

Happy, happy, there she lies!
   Thou shalt feel the lash no more;
Thus full many a Negro dies
   Ere we reach the destined shore.

Driven like cattle to a fair,
   See they sell us, young and old;
Child from mother too they tear,
   All for love of filthy gold.

William Blake

'The Chimney-Sweeper' (*Innocence* and *Experience* versions), 'The Lamb' and 'The Tiger', from *Songs of Innocence and of Experience* (1794); extract from a letter to Reverend Trusler (1799); extracts from 'Auguries of Innocence' (c. 1803)

One of the seminal exponents of Romanticism, Blake was a fiercely independent poet, engraver and painter. The *Songs* aim to show the contrasting states of the human soul, and are succinct expressions of psychological, spiritual and social observation. The four poems here typify the vivid contrasts and tensions.

In the extract from a letter to Reverend Trusler, Blake seeks – in typically confident, adversarial style – to convince a rather more conventional cleric of the truth of his own world view.

The extracts from 'Auguries of Innocence' illustrate the development of Blake's powerful sense of what it means to be human.

The Chimney-Sweeper
(*Innocence* version)

When my mother died I was very young,
And my father sold me while yet my tongue
Could scarcely cry, 'weep weep weep weep'.
So your chimneys I sweep and in soot I sleep.

There's little Tom Dacre, who cried when his head,
That curled like a lamb's back, was shaved, so I said:
'Hush Tom, never mind it, for when your head's bare,
You know that the soot cannot spoil your white hair.'

And so he was quiet, and that very night,
As Tom was a-sleeping, he had such a sight:
That thousands of sweepers, Dick, Joe, Ned and Jack,
Were all of them locked up in coffins of black,

And by came an angel who had a bright key,
And he opened the coffins and set them all free.
Then down a green plain leaping, laughing they run,
And wash in a river and shine in the sun.

Then naked and white, all their bags left behind,
They rise upon clouds, and sport in the wind.
And the angel told Tom if he'd be a good boy,
He'd have God for his father and never want joy.

And so Tom awoke, and we rose in the dark,
And got with our bags and our brushes to work.
Though the morning was cold, Tom was happy and warm.
So if all do their duty, they need not fear harm.

The Chimney-Sweeper
(*Experience* version)

A little black thing among the snow,
Crying 'weep, weep' in notes of woe!
'Where are thy father and mother? Say!'
'They are both gone up to the church to pray.

'Because I was happy upon the heath,
And smiled among the winter's snow,
They clothèd me in the clothes of death,
And taught me to sing the notes of woe.

'And because I am happy and dance and sing,
They think they have done me no injury,
And are gone to praise God and his priest and king,
Who make up a heaven of our misery.'

The Lamb

Little Lamb who made thee?
Dost thou know who made thee?
Gave thee life and bid thee feed
By the stream and o'er the mead;
Gave thee clothing of delight,
Softest clothing woolly bright;
Gave thee such a tender voice,
Making all the vales rejoice.
Little Lamb who made thee?
Dost thou know who made thee?

Little Lamb I'll tell thee,
Little Lamb I'll tell thee:
He is callèd by thy name,
For he calls himself a lamb.
He is meek and he is mild;
He became a little child.
I a child and thou a lamb,
We are callèd by his name.
Little Lamb God bless thee.
Little Lamb God bless thee.

The Tiger

Tiger, Tiger, burning bright
In the forests of the night,
What immortal hand or eye
Dare frame thy fearful symmetry?

Burnt in distant deeps or skies
The cruel fire of thine eyes?
On what wings dare he aspire?
What the hand dare seize the fire?

And what shoulder and what art
Could twist the sinews of thy heart?
And when thy heart began to beat
What dread hand and what dread feet

Could fetch it from the furnace deep
And in thy horrid ribs dare steep
In the well of sanguine woe?
In what clay and in what mould
Were thy eyes of fury roll'd?

Where the hammer? Where the chain?
In what furnace was thy brain?
What the anvil? What dread grasp
Dare its deadly terrors clasp?

When the stars threw down their spears
And water'd heaven with their tears
Dare he laugh his work to see?
Dare he who made the lamb make thee?

Tiger, Tiger, burning bright
In the forests of the night,
What immortal hand and eye
Dare frame thy fearful symmetry?

Extract from a letter to Reverend Trusler

Fun I love but too much Fun is of all things the most loathsom. Mirth
is better than Fun, & Happiness is better than Mirth. I feel that a Man
may be happy in This World. And I know that This World Is a World of
Imagination & Vision. I see Every thing I paint In This World, but Every
body does not see alike. To the Eyes of a Miser a Guinea is far more
beautiful than the Sun, & a bag worn with the use of Money has more
beautiful proportions than a Vine filled with Grapes. The tree which
moves some to tears of joy is in the Eyes of others only a Green thing
which stands in the way. Some see Nature all Ridicule & Deformity, &
by these I shall not regulate my proportions; & some scarce see
Nature at all. But to the Eyes of the Man of Imagination, Nature is
Imagination itself. As a man is, so he sees. As the Eye is formed, such
are its Powers. You certainly Mistake, when you say that the Visions
of Fancy are not to be found in This World. To Me This World is all
One continued Vision of Fancy or Imagination, & I feel Flatter'd when

I am told so. What is it sets Homer, Virgil & Milton in so high a rank of Art? Why is the Bible more Entertaining & Instructive than any other book? Is it not because they are addressed to the Imagination, which is Spiritual Sensation, & but mediately to the Understanding or Reason? Such is True Painting, and such was alone valued by the Greeks & the best modern Artists. Consider what Lord Bacon says: 'Sense sends over to Imagination before Reason have judged, & Reason sends over to Imagination before the Decree can be acted.' See Advancement of Learning, Part 2 P. 47 of first Edition.

But I am happy to find a Great Majority of Fellow Mortals who can Elucidate My Visions, & Particularly they have been Elucidated by Children, who have taken a greater delight in contemplating my Pictures than I even hoped. Neither Youth nor Childhood is Folly or Incapacity. Some Children are Fools & so are some Old Men. But There is a vast Majority on the side of Imagination or Spiritual Sensation.

Auguries of Innocence

To see a world in a grain of sand
And a heaven in a wild flower,
Hold infinity in the palm of your hand
And eternity in an hour.
A robin redbreast in a cage
Puts all Heaven in a rage,
A dove-house filled with doves and pigeons
Shudders Hell through all its regions.
A dog starved at his master's gate
Predicts the ruin of the state.
A horse misused upon the road
Calls to Heaven for human blood.
Each outcry of the hunted hare
A fibre from the brain does tear.
A skylark wounded in the wing,
A cherubim does cease to sing.
The gamecock clipped and armed for fight
Does the rising sun affright.
Every wolf's and lion's howl
Raises from Hell a human soul.
The wild deer wandering here and there
Keeps the human soul from care.
The lamb misused breeds public strife,
And yet forgives the butcher's knife.
The bat that flits at close of eve

Has left the brain that won't believe.
The owl that calls upon the night
Speaks the unbeliever's fright.
He who shall hurt the little wren
Shall never be beloved by men.
He who the ox to wrath has moved
Shall never be by woman loved.
The wanton boy that kills the fly
Shall feel the spider's enmity.
He who torments the chafer's sprite
Weaves a bower in endless night.
The caterpillar on the leaf
Repeats to thee thy mother's grief.
Kill not the moth nor butterfly,
For the Last Judgement draweth nigh.
He who shall train the horse to war
Shall never pass the polar bar.
The beggar's dog and widow's cat –
Feed them and thou wilt grow fat.
The gnat that sings his summer's song
Poison gets from slander's tongue.
The poison of the snake and newt
Is the sweat of envy's foot;
The poison of the honey bee
Is the artist's jealousy.
The prince's robes and beggar's rags
Are toadstools on the miser's bags.
A truth that's told with bad intent
Beats all the lies you can invent.
It is right it should be so;
Man was made for joy and woe,
And when this we rightly know
Through the world we safely go.
Joy and woe are woven fine,
A clothing for the soul divine.
Under every grief and pine
Runs a joy with silken twine.
...
If the sun and moon should doubt
They'd immediately go out.
To be in a passion you good may do,
But no good if a passion is in you.
The whore and gambler by the state

Licenced build that nation's fate.
The harlot's cry from street to street
Shall weave old England's winding sheet;
The winner's shout, the loser's curse
Dance before dead England's hearse.
Every night and every morn
Some to misery are born;
Every morn and every night
Some are born to sweet delight.
Some are born to sweet delight,
Some are born to endless night.
We are led to believe a lie
When we see not through the eye,
Which was born in a night to perish in a night,
When the soul slept in beams of light.
God appears and God is light
To those poor souls who dwell in night,
But does a human form display
To those who dwell in realms of day.

Mary Wollstonecraft

'A Revolution in Female Manners' from *A Vindication of the Rights of Woman* (1792)

Wollstonecraft is now hailed as one of the founders of feminism, but was widely reviled in her day: strange, perhaps, to modern readers, who are often struck by her thoughtful, reasonable and conciliatory approach, typified in this extract.

Let not men then in the pride of power use the same arguments that tyrannic kings and venal ministers have used, and fallaciously assert that woman ought to be subjected because she has always been so. But when man, governed by reasonable laws, enjoys his natural freedom, let him despise woman if she do not share it with him – and, till that glorious period arrives, in descanting on the folly of the sex, let him not overlook his own.

Women, it is true, obtaining power by unjust means by practising or fostering vice, evidently lose the rank which reason would assign them, and they become either abject slaves or capricious tyrants. They lose all simplicity, all dignity of mind, in acquiring power, and act as men are observed to act when they have been exalted by the same means.

It is time to effect a revolution in female manners, time to restore to them their lost dignity, and make them (as a part of the human species) labour, by reforming themselves, to reform the world. It is time to separate unchangeable morals from local manners. If men be demi-gods, why let us serve them! And if the dignity of the female soul be as disputable as that of animals; if their reason does not afford sufficient light to direct their conduct whilst unerring instinct is denied, they are surely of all creatures the most miserable, and, bent beneath the iron hand of destiny, must submit to be a fair defect in creation. But to justify the ways of providence respecting them, by pointing out some irrefragable reason for thus making such a large portion of mankind accountable and not accountable, would puzzle the subtlest casuist.

William Wordsworth

'Lines Written a Few Miles above Tintern Abbey, on Revisiting the Banks of the Wye During a Tour, 13 July 1798'; 'Song' (1798); extracts from the revised Preface (1802) to *Lyrical Ballads*

'Lines Written a Few Miles above Tintern Abbey', from *Lyrical Ballads*, meditative and melancholy as it is, may be seen as a centrepiece among Romantic texts, just as Wordsworth himself is a central Romantic figure. The tensions between creativity and conventionality pervade all his work. Contrastingly brief, 'Song', also from *Lyrical Ballads*, seems magically evocative of the subject, Lucy.

The Preface to *Lyrical Ballads* is one of the most significant statements about the nature of poetry to emerge from the Romantic era, and its influence is still widely felt.

Lines Written a Few Miles above Tintern Abbey

Five years have passed; five summers, with the length
Of five long winters! And again I hear
These waters, rolling from their mountain springs
With a sweet inland murmur. Once again
Do I behold these steep and lofty cliffs,
Which on a wild secluded scene impress
Thoughts of more deep seclusion, and connect
The landscape with the quiet of the sky.
The day is come when I again repose
Here, under this dark sycamore, and view
These plots of cottage-ground, these orchard-tufts,
Which, at this season, with their unripe fruits,
Among the woods and copses lose themselves,
Nor, with their green and simple hue, disturb

The wild green landscape. Once again I see
These hedgerows – hardly hedgerows, little lines
Of sportive wood run wild; these pastoral farms
Green to the very door; and wreaths of smoke
Sent up in silence from among the trees,
With some uncertain notice, as might seem,
Of vagrant dwellers in the houseless woods,
Or of some hermit's cave, where by his fire
The hermit sits alone.
                                    Though absent long,
These forms of beauty have not been to me
As is a landscape to a blind man's eye;
But oft, in lonely rooms, and mid the din
Of towns and cities, I have owed to them,
In hours of weariness, sensations sweet,
Felt in the blood, and felt along the heart,
And passing even into my purer mind
With tranquil restoration; feelings too
Of unremembered pleasure – such, perhaps,
As may have had no trivial influence
On that best portion of a good man's life,
His little, nameless, unremembered acts
Of kindness and of love. Nor less, I trust,
To them I may have owed another gift,
Of aspect more sublime; that blessed mood
In which the burden of the mystery,
In which the heavy and the weary weight
Of all this unintelligible world
Is lightened – that serene and blessed mood
In which the affections gently lead us on
Until the breath of this corporeal frame
And even the motion of our human blood
Almost suspended, we are laid asleep
In body, and become a living soul,
While with an eye made quiet by the power
Of harmony, and the deep power of joy,
We see into the life of things.
                                    If this
Be but a vain belief – yet oh, how oft
In darkness, and amid the many shapes
Of joyless daylight, when the fretful stir
Unprofitable, and the fever of the world,
Have hung upon the beatings of my heart,

How oft, in spirit, have I turned to thee,
Oh sylvan Wye! Thou wanderer through the woods,
How often has my spirit turned to thee!
   And now, with gleams of half-extinguished thought,
With many recognitions dim and faint
And somewhat of a sad perplexity,
The picture of the mind revives again;
While here I stand, not only with the sense
Of present pleasure, but with pleasing thoughts
That in this moment there is life and food
For future years. And so I dare to hope,
Though changed, no doubt, from what I was when first
I came among these hills, when like a roe
I bounded o'er the mountains by the sides
Of the deep rivers and the lonely streams
Wherever nature led, more like a man
Flying from something that he dreads than one
Who sought the thing he loved. For nature then
(The coarser pleasures of my boyish days
And their glad animal movements all gone by)
To me was all in all.
                    I cannot paint
What then I was. The sounding cataract
Haunted me like a passion; the tall rock,
The mountain, and the deep and gloomy wood,
Their colours and their forms, were then to me
An appetite, a feeling and a love
That had no need of a remoter charm
By thought supplied, or any interest
Unborrowed from the eye. That time is past,
And all its aching joys are now no more,
And all its dizzy raptures. Not for this
Faint I, nor mourn, nor murmur; other gifts
Have followed – for such loss, I would believe,
Abundant recompense. For I have learned
To look on nature not as in the hour
Of thoughtless youth, but hearing oftentimes
The still, sad music of humanity,
Not harsh nor grating, though of ample power
To chasten and subdue. And I have felt
A presence that disturbs me with the joy
Of elevated thoughts, a sense sublime
Of something far more deeply interfused,

Whose dwelling is the light of setting suns,
And the round ocean, and the living air,
And the blue sky, and in the mind of man –
A motion and a spirit that impels
All thinking things, all objects of all thought,
And rolls through all things. Therefore am I still
A lover of the meadows and the woods
And mountains, and of all that we behold
From this green earth, of all the mighty world
Of eye and ear (both what they half-create
And what perceive) – well-pleased to recognize
In nature and the language of the sense,
The anchor of my purest thoughts, the nurse,
The guide, the guardian of my heart, and soul
Of all my moral being.
                    Nor, perchance,
If I were not thus taught, should I the more
Suffer my genial spirits to decay;
For thou art with me, here, upon the banks
Of this fair river – thou, my dearest friend,
My dear, dear friend, and in thy voice I catch
The language of my former heart, and read
My former pleasures in the shooting lights
Of thy wild eyes. Oh, yet a little while
May I behold in thee what I was once,
My dear, dear sister! And this prayer I make,
Knowing that Nature never did betray
The heart that loved her; 'tis her privilege,
Through all the years of this our life, to lead
From joy to joy, for she can so inform
The mind that is within us, so impress
With quietness and beauty, and so feed
With lofty thoughts, that neither evil tongues,
Rash judgements, nor the sneers of selfish men,
Nor greetings where no kindness is, nor all
The dreary intercourse of daily life,
Shall e'er prevail against us, or disturb
Our cheerful faith that all which we behold
Is full of blessings. Therefore let the moon
Shine on thee in thy solitary walk,
And let the misty mountain-winds be free
To blow against thee. And in after-years,
When these wild ecstasies shall be matured

Into a sober pleasure, when thy mind
Shall be a mansion for all lovely forms,
Thy memory be as a dwelling-place
For all sweet sounds and harmonies – oh then
If solitude, or fear, or pain, or grief
Should be thy portion, with what healing thoughts
Of tender joy wilt thou remember me,
And these my exhortations! Nor perchance,
If I should be where I no more can hear
Thy voice, nor catch from thy wild eyes these gleams
Of past existence, wilt thou then forget
That on the banks of this delightful stream
We stood together; and that I, so long
A worshipper of nature, hither came
Unwearied in that service – rather say
With warmer love, oh with far deeper zeal
Of holier love! Nor wilt thou then forget
That, after many wanderings, many years
Of absence, these steep woods and lofty cliffs
And this green pastoral landscape, were to me
More dear, both for themselves, and for thy sake.

Song

She dwelt among th' untrodden ways
    Beside the springs of Dove,
A maid whom there were none to praise
    And very few to love.

A violet by a mossy stone
    Half-hidden from the eye,
Fair as a star when only one
    Is shining in the sky!

She *lived* unknown, and few could know
    When Lucy ceased to be;
But she is in her grave, and oh!
    The difference to me.

From the Preface to Lyrical Ballads

The principal object, then, which I proposed to myself in these
poems, was to choose incidents and situations from common life,
and to relate or describe them throughout, as far as was possible, in

a selection of language really used by men, and at the same time to throw over them a certain colouring of imagination, whereby ordinary things should be presented to the mind in an unusual way. And further, and above all, to make these incidents and situations interesting by tracing in them (truly, though not ostentatiously) the primary laws of our nature, chiefly as far as regards the manner in which we associate ideas in a state of excitement.

Low and rustic life was generally chosen because in that condition the essential passions of the heart find a better soil in which they can attain their maturity, are less under restraint, and speak a plainer and more emphatic language; because in that condition of life our elementary feelings coexist in a state of greater simplicity, and consequently may be more accurately contemplated and more forcibly communicated; because the manners of rural life germinate from those elementary feelings, and (from the necessary character of rural occupations) are more easily comprehended and are more durable; and, lastly, because in that condition the passions of men are incorporated with the beautiful and permanent forms of nature.

The language, too, of these men is adopted (purified indeed from what appear to be its real defects – from all lasting and rational causes of dislike or disgust) because such men hourly communicate with the best objects from which the best part of language is originally derived, and because, from their rank in society and the sameness and narrow circle of their intercourse being less under the influence of social vanity, they convey their feelings and notions in simple and unelaborated expressions. Accordingly, such a language, arising out of repeated experience and regular feelings, is a more permanent and a far more philosophical language than that which is frequently substituted for it by poets who think that they are conferring honour upon themselves and their art, in proportion as they separate themselves from the sympathies of men and indulge in arbitrary and capricious habits of expression, in order to furnish food for fickle tastes and fickle appetites of their own creation. ...

Poetry is the image of man and nature. The obstacles which stand in the way of the fidelity of the biographer and historian (and of their consequent utility) are incalculably greater than those which are to be encountered by the poet who has an adequate notion of the dignity of his art. The poet writes under one restriction only – namely, that of the necessity of giving immediate pleasure to a human being possessed of that information which may be expected from him, not as a lawyer, a physician, a mariner, an astronomer, or a natural philosopher, but as a man. Except this one restriction, there is no object standing between the poet and the image of things; between this, and the biographer and historian, there are a thousand.

Nor let this necessity of producing immediate pleasure be considered as a degradation of the poet's art; it is far otherwise. It is an acknowledgement of the beauty of the universe, an acknowledgement the more sincere because it is not formal, but indirect; it is a task light and easy to him who looks at the world in the spirit of love. Further, it is a homage paid to the native and naked dignity of man, to the grand elementary principle of pleasure by which he knows, and feels, and lives, and moves ...

I have said that poetry is the spontaneous overflow of powerful feelings; it takes its origin from emotion recollected in tranquillity. The emotion is contemplated till, by a species of reaction, the tranquillity gradually disappears, and an emotion kindred to that which was before the subject of contemplation is gradually produced, and does itself actually exist in the mind. In this mood successful composition generally begins, and in a mood similar to this it is carried on. But the emotion (of whatever kind and in whatever degree) from various causes is qualified by various pleasures, so that in describing any passions whatsoever which are voluntarily described, the mind will upon the whole be in a state of enjoyment. Now, if nature be thus cautious in preserving in a state of enjoyment a being thus employed, the poet ought to profit by the lesson thus held forth to him, and ought especially to take care of that, whatever passions he communicates to his reader, those passions (if his reader's mind be sound and vigorous) should always be accompanied with an overbalance of pleasure.

Dorothy Wordsworth

Extracts from *The Grasmere Journals* (1801–1802)

For so long overshadowed by her illustrious brother, there has been something of a critical reappraisal of Dorothy Wordsworth's writing; these brief extracts give a subtle flavour of her observant, sensitively felt art.

Sunday 22nd [November]. – We wrote to Coleridge – sent our letter by the Boy. Mr and Miss Simpson came in at tea time. We went with them to the Blacksmith's and returned by Butterlip How – a frost and wind with bright moonshine. The vale looked spacious and very beautiful – the level meadows seemed very large, and some nearer us unequal ground heaving like sand, the Cottages beautiful and quiet. We passed one near which stood a cropped ash with upright forked Branches like the Devil's horns frightening a guilty conscience. We were happy and chearful when we came home – we went early to bed.

Tuesday 24th [November] ... John Green's house looked pretty under Silver How. As we were going along we were stopped at once, at the distance perhaps of 50 yards from our favorite Birch tree. It was yielding to the gusty wind with all its tender twigs, the sun shone upon it and it glanced in the wind like a flying sunshiny shower. It was a tree in shape with stem and branches but it was like a Spirit of water. The sun went in and it resumed its purplish appearance the twigs still yielding to the wind but not so visibly to us. The other Birch trees that were near it looked bright and chearful, but it was a creature by its own self among them. We could not get into Mr Gell's grounds – the old tree fallen from its undue exaltation above the Gate. A shower came on when we were at Benson's. We went through the wood – it became fair – there was a rainbow which spanned the lake from the Island house to the foot of Bainriggs. The village looked populous and beautiful. Catkins are coming out palm trees budding – the alder with its plumb coloured buds. We came home over the stepping stones. The Lake was foamy with white waves. *I* saw a solitary butter flower in the wood. I found it not easy to get over the stepping stones. Reached home at dinner time. ...

Tuesday 29th [December]. A fine morning. A thin fog upon the hills which soon disappeared. The sun shone. Wilkinson went with us to the top of the hill. We turned out of the road at the 2nd mile stone and passed a pretty cluster of houses at the foot of St John's Vale. The houses were among tall trees partly of Scotch fir, and some naked forest trees. We crossed a Bridge just below these houses and the river winded sweetly along the meadows. Our road soon led us along the sides of dreary bare hills, but we had a glorious prospect to the left of Saddleback, half way covered with snow and underneath the comfortable white houses and the village of Threlkeld. These houses and the village want trees about them. Skiddaw was behind us and dear Coleridge's desert home – As we ascended the hills it grew very cold and slippery. Luckily the wind was at our backs and helped us on. A sharp hail shower gathered at the head of Matterdale and the view upwards was very grand – the wild cottages seen through the hurrying hail shower. The wind drove and eddied about and about and the hills looked large and swelling through the storm. We thought of Coleridge. O the bonny nooks and windings and curlings of the Beck down at the bottom of the steep green mossy Banks. ...

Thursday 18th [March] As we came along Ambleside vale in the twilight – it was a grave evening – there was something in the air that compelled me to serious thought. The hills were large, closed in by the sky. It was nearly dark when I parted from the Lloyds that is,

night was come on and the moon was overcast. But as I climbed
Moss the moon came out from behind a mountain mass of Black
clouds – O the unutterable darkness of the sky and the earth below
the moon! and the glorious brightness of the moon itself! There was
a vivid sparkling streak of light at this end of Rydale water but the
rest was very dark and Loughrigg fell and Silver How were white and
bright as if they were covered with hoar frost. The moon retired again
and appeared and disappeared several times before I reached home.
Once there was no moonlight to be seen but upon the Island house
and the promontory of the Island where it stands, 'That needs must
be a holy place' etc. etc. I had many very exquisite feelings and when I
saw this lowly Building in the waters among the Dark and lofty hills,
with that bright soft light upon it, it made me more than half a poet. I
was tired when I reached home. I could not sit down to reading and
tried to write verses but alas! I gave up expecting William and went
soon to bed. Fletcher's carts came home late.

Samuel Taylor Coleridge

'Kubla Khan' (1797); extracts from *Biographia Literaria* (1817); Conversation
poems: 'The Eolian Harp' and 'This Lime-Tree Bower My Prison' (1797)

Coleridge's fragile, damaged genius is nowhere better demonstrated than in the
highly enigmatic 'Kubla Khan' (and its equally enigmatic preface), which has
certainly entered the mythology of Romanticism.

In the extracts from *Biographia Literaria* are more seminal thoughts on the
nature of Romantic creativity, as Coleridge reflects on his life and art.

Coleridge is in different mode with the wistful lyricism of the two 'Conversation
poems'. The second of the poems, 'This Lime-Tree Bower My Prison' was written in
the June of 1797, when some long-expected friends paid a visit to the author's
cottage. On the morning of their arrival, Coleridge met with an accident which
disabled him from walking during their stay. One evening, when they had left him
for a few hours, he composed the lines in the garden bower.

Kubla Khan

In Xanadu did Kubla Khan
A stately pleasure-dome decree:
Where Alph, the sacred river, ran
Through caverns measureless to man
Down to a sunless sea.
So twice five miles of fertile ground
With walls and towers were girdled round:

And here were gardens bright with sinuous rills
Where blossomed many an incense-bearing tree;
And here were forests ancient as the hills,
Enfolding sunny spots of greenery.
But oh, that deep romantic chasm which slanted
Down a green hill athwart a cedarn cover!
A savage place! as holy and enchanted
As e'er beneath a waning moon was haunted
By woman wailing for her demon-lover!
And from this chasm, with ceaseless turmoil seething,
As if this earth in fast thick pants were breathing,
A mighty fountain momently was forced:
Amid whose swift half-intermitted burst
Huge fragments vaulted like rebounding hail,
Or chaffy grain beneath the thresher's flail:
And 'mid these dancing rocks at once and ever,
It flung up momently the sacred river.
Five miles meandering with a mazy motion
Through wood and dale the sacred river ran,
Then reached the caverns measureless to man.
And sank in tumult to a lifeless ocean:
And 'mid this tumult Kubla heard from far
Ancestral voices prophesying war!
    The shadow of the dome of pleasure
      Floated midway on the waves;
    Where was heard the mingled measure
      From the fountain and the caves.
It was a miracle of rare device,
A sunny pleasure-dome with caves of ice!

      A damsel with a dulcimer
      In a vision once I saw:
      It was an Abyssinian maid
      And on her dulcimer she played,
      Singing of Mount Abora.
      Could I revive within me
      Her symphony and song,
      To such a deep delight 'twould win me,
That with music loud and long,
I would build that dome in air,
That sunny dome! those caves of ice!
And all who heard should see them there,
And all should cry, Beware! Beware!

His flashing eyes, his floating hair!
Weave a circle round him thrice,
And close your eyes with holy dread:
For he on honey-dew hath fed
And drunk the milk of Paradise.

*This fragment with a good deal more, not recoverable, composed in a
sort of reverie brought on by two grains of opium taken to check a
dysentery, at a farm-house between Porlock and Lynton, a quarter of
a mile from Culbone Church, in the fall of the year 1797.*
S.T. Coleridge

Extracts from Biographia Literaria

The imagination then I consider either as primary or secondary. The
primary imagination I hold to be the living power and prime agent of
all human perception, and as a repetition in the finite mind of the
eternal act of creation in the infinite I AM. The secondary imagination
I consider as an echo of the former, coexisting with the conscious will,
yet still as identical with the primary in the *kind* of its agency, and
differing only in *degree*, and in the *mode* of its operation. It dissolves,
diffuses, dissipates, in order to recreate; or, where this process is
rendered impossible, yet still at all events it struggles to idealise and
to unify. It is essentially *vital*, even as all objects (*as* objects) are
essentially fixed and dead.

Fancy, on the contrary, has no other counters to play with but
fixities and definites. The fancy is language of *real* life. From this
Preface, prefixed to poems in which it was impossible to deny the
presence of original genius (however mistaken its direction might be
deemed), arose the whole long-continued controversy. For, from the
conjunction of perceived power with supposed heresy, I explain the
inveteracy and (in some instances, I grieve to say) the acrimonious
passions with which the controversy has been conducted by the
assailants. …

'What is poetry?' is so nearly the same question with 'what is a
poet?' that the answer to the one is involved in the solution of the
other. For it is a distinction resulting from the poetic genius itself,
which sustains and modifies the images, thoughts, and emotions of
the poet's own mind. The poet, described in ideal perfection, brings
the whole soul of man into activity, with the subordination of its
faculties to each other, according to their relative worth and dignity.
He diffuses a tone and spirit of unity that blends and (as it were)
fuses each into each by that synthetic and magical power to which I

would exclusively appropriate the name of imagination. This power, first put in action by the will and understanding, and retained under their irremissive, though gentle and unnoticed, control ... reveals itself in the balance or reconcilement of opposite or discordant qualities; of sameness with difference; of the general with the concrete; the idea with the image; the individual with the representative; the sense of novelty and freshness, with old and familiar objects; a more than usual state of emotion, with more than usual order; judgement ever awake and steady self-possession, with enthusiasm and feeling profound or vehement – and, while it blends and harmonizes the natural and the artificial, still subordinates art to nature; the manner to the matter; and our admiration of the poet to our sympathy with the poetry.

The Eolian Harp

My pensive Sara, thy soft cheek reclined
Thus on mine arm, most soothing sweet it is
To sit beside our cot, our cot o'ergrown
With white-flowered jasmine and the broad-leaved myrtle
(Meet emblems they of innocence and love),
And watch the clouds that late were rich with light
Slow-sad'ning round, and mark the star of eve
Serenely brilliant (such should wisdom be)
Shine opposite! How exquisite the scents
Snatched from yon bean-field! And the world so hushed!
The stilly murmur of the distant sea
Tells us of silence.
     And that simplest lute
Placed lengthways in the clasping casement – hark
How by the desultory breeze caressed!
Like some coy maid half-yielding to her lover,
It pours such sweet upbraidings as must needs
Tempt to repeat the wrong. And now its strings
Boldlier swept, the long sequacious notes
Over delicious surges sink and rise,
Such a soft floating witchery of sound
As twilight elfins make when they at eve
Voyage on gentle gales from fairyland,
Where melodies round honey-dropping flowers
Footless and wild, like birds of paradise,
Nor pause nor perch, hovering on untamed wing.
Oh the one life within us and abroad,

Which meets all motion and becomes its soul,
A light in sound, a sound-like power in light,
Rhythm in all thought, and joyance everywhere –
Methinks it should have been impossible
Not to love all things in a world so filled,
Where the breeze warbles, and the mute still air
Is Music slumbering on its instrument!
    And thus, my love, as on the midway slope
Of yonder hill I stretch my limbs at noon,
Whilst through my half-closed eyelids I behold
The sunbeams dance, like diamonds, on the main,
And tranquil muse upon tranquillity,
Full many a thought uncalled and undetained,
And many idle flitting fantasies
Traverse my indolent and passive brain –
As wild and various as the random gales
That swell and flutter on this subject lute!
    And what if all of animated nature
Be but organic harps diversely framed,
That tremble into thought, as o'er them sweeps,
Plastic and vast, one intellectual breeze,
At once the soul of each, and God of all?
    But thy more serious eye a mild reproof
Darts, oh beloved woman! – nor such thoughts
Dim and unhallowed dost thou not reject,
And biddest me walk humbly with my God.
Meek daughter in the family of Christ,
Well hast thou said and holily dispraised
These shapings of the unregenerate mind,
Bubbles that glitter as they rise and break
On vain philosophy's aye-babbling spring.
For never guiltless may I speak of Him,
Th' Incomprehensible! save when with awe
I praise him, and with faith that inly feels –
Who with his saving mercies healed me,
A sinful and most miserable man
Wildered and dark, and gave me to possess
Peace, and this cot, and thee, heart-honoured maid!

This Lime-Tree Bower My Prison

Well, they are gone, and here must I remain,
This lime-tree bower my prison! I have lost

Beauties and feelings, such as would have been
Most sweet to my remembrance even when age
Had dimmed mine eyes to blindness! They, meanwhile,
Friends whom I never more may meet again,
On springy heath, along the hilltop edge,
Wander in gladness, and wind down, perchance,
To that still roaring dell of which I told;
The roaring dell, o'erwooded, narrow, deep,
And only speckled by the midday sun;
Where its slim trunk the ash from rock to rock
Flings arching like a bridge – that branchless ash,
Unsunned and damp, whose few poor yellow leaves
Ne'er tremble in the gale, yet tremble still,
Fanned by the waterfall! And there my friends
Behold the dark green file of long lank weeds,
That all at once (a most fantastic sight!)
Still nod and drip beneath the dripping edge
Of the blue clay-stone.
                   Now, my friends emerge
Beneath thy wide wide heaven – and view again
The many-steepled tract magnificent
Of hilly fields and meadows, and the sea,
With some fair bark, perhaps, whose sails light up
The slip of smooth clear blue betwixt two isles
Of purple shadow! Yes, they wander on
In gladness all – but thou, methinks, most glad,
My gentle-hearted Charles! For thou hast pined
And hungered after nature many a year
In the great city pent, winning thy way,
With sad yet patient soul, through evil and pain
And strange calamity! Ah, slowly sink
Behind the western ridge, thou glorious sun!
Shine in the slant beams of the sinking orb,
Ye purple heath-flowers! Richlier burn, ye clouds!
Live in the yellow light, ye distant groves!
And kindle, thou blue ocean! So my friend,
Struck with deep joy, may stand, as I have stood,
Silent with swimming sense; yea, gazing round
On the wide landscape, gaze till all doth seem
Less gross than bodily, and of such hues
As veil the Almighty Spirit, when yet he makes
Spirits perceive His presence.
                     A delight

Comes sudden on my heart, and I am glad
As I myself were there! Nor in this bower,
This little lime-tree bower, have I not marked
Much that has soothed me. Pale beneath the blaze
Hung the transparent foliage; and I watched
Some broad and sunny leaf, and loved to see
The shadow of the leaf and stem above
Dappling its sunshine! And that walnut tree
Was richly tinged, and a deep radiance lay
Full on the ancient ivy which *usurps*
Those fronting elms, and now with blackest mass
Makes their dark branches gleam a lighter hue
Through the late twilight; and though now the bat
Wheels silent by, and not a swallow twitters,
Yet still the solitary humble-bee
Sings in the bean-flower! Henceforth I shall know
That nature ne'er deserts the wise and pure –
No scene so narrow but may well employ
Each faculty of sense, and keep the heart
Awake to love and beauty! And sometimes
'Tis well to be bereaved of promised good,
That we may lift the soul, and contemplate
With lively joy the joys we cannot share.
My gentle-hearted Charles! when the last rook
Beat its straight path along the dusky air
Homewards, I blessed it, deeming its black wing
(Now a dim speck, now vanishing in the light)
Had crossed the mighty orb's dilated glory
While thou stoodst gazing; or, when all was still,
Flew creaking o'er thy head, and had a charm
For thee, my gentle-hearted Charles! to whom
No sound is dissonant which tells of Life.

George Gordon (Lord) Byron

'She Walks in Beauty' (1814) and 'When We Two Parted' (1815)

'Mad, bad, and dangerous to know', as Lady Caroline Lamb famously described Byron – and his reputation in life matched the description. Ironically, perhaps, there is an appealingly quiet charm in the poems presented here.

She Walks in Beauty

I

She walks in beauty like the night
  Of cloudless climes and starry skies,
And all that's best of dark and bright
  Meet in her aspect and her eyes,
Thus mellowed to that tender light
  Which heaven to gaudy day denies.

II

One shade the more, one ray the less
  Had half-impaired the nameless grace
Which waves in every raven tress
  Or softly lightens o'er her face –
Where thoughts serenely sweet express
  How pure, how dear their dwelling place.

III

And on that cheek and o'er that brow,
  So soft, so calm, yet eloquent,
The smiles that win, the tints that glow,
  But tell of days in goodness spent,
A mind at peace with all below,
  A heart whose love is innocent.

When We Two Parted

1

When we two parted
  In silence and tears,
Half broken-hearted,
  To sever for years,
Pale grew thy cheek and cold,
  Colder thy kiss –
Truly that hour foretold
  Sorrow to this.

2

The dew of the morning
  Sunk chill on my brow –
It felt like the warning
  Of what I feel now.
Thy vows are all broken,

And light is thy fame;
I hear thy name spoken,
  And share in its shame.

        3
They name thee before me –
  A knell to mine ear;
A shudder comes o'er me –
  Why wert thou so dear?
They know not I knew thee,
  Who knew thee too well;
Long, long shall I rue thee,
  Too deeply to tell.

        4
In secret we met,
  In silence I grieve
That thy heart could forget,
  Thy spirit deceive.
If I should meet thee
  After long years,
How should I greet thee?
  With silence and tears.

Percy Bysshe Shelley

'Ode to the West Wind' (1819); extract from 'On Life' (1819)

Dramatic is perhaps the word that best describes the poetry of Shelley: a lightness
of touch belying profundity of thought and aptness of expression. This 'Ode', from
Prometheus Unbound, typifies these qualities.

Sharply perceptive, the passage from 'On Life' is also notable for its references
to Shakespeare and Milton – Romantic heroes much read and admired by both
Shelleys.

Ode to the West Wind

                I
Oh wild west wind, thou breath of autumn's being;
Thou from those unseen presence the leaves dead
Are driven, like ghosts from an enchanter fleeing,

Yellow, and black, and pale, and hectic red,
Pestilence-stricken multitudes; oh thou
Who chariotest to their dark wintry bed

The winged seeds, where they lie cold and low,
Each like a corpse within its grave, until
Thine azure sister of the spring shall blow

Her clarion o'er the dreaming earth, and fill
(Driving sweet buds like flocks to feed in air)
With living hues and odours plain and hill –

Wild spirit, which art moving everywhere,
Destroyer and preserver, hear, oh hear!

II

Thou on whose stream, mid the steep sky's commotion,
Loose clouds like earth's decaying leaves are shed,
Shook from the tangled boughs of heaven and ocean,

Angels of rain and lightning; there are spread
On the blue surface of thine airy surge,
Like the bright hair uplifted from the head

Of some fierce maenad, even from the dim verge
Of the horizon to the zenith's height,
The locks of the approaching storm. Thou dirge

Of the dying year, to which this closing night
Will be the dome of a vast sepulchre,
Vaulted with all thy congregated might

Of vapours, from whose solid atmosphere
Black rain, and fire, and hail will burst – oh hear!

III

Thou who didst waken from his summer dreams
The blue Mediterranean, where he lay,
Lulled by the coil of his crystalline streams,

Beside a pumice isle in Baiae's bay,
And saw in sleep old palaces and towers
Quivering within the wave's intenser day,

All overgrown with azure moss and flowers
So sweet, the sense faints picturing them! Thou
For whose path the Atlantic's level powers

Cleave themselves into chasms, while far below
The sea-blooms and the oozy woods which wear
The sapless foliage of the ocean, know

Thy voice, and suddenly grow grey with fear,
And tremble and despoil themselves – oh hear!

IV

If I were a dead leaf thou mightest bear;
If I were a swift cloud to fly with thee;
A wave to pant beneath thy power, and share

The impulse of thy strength, only less free
Than thou, oh uncontrollable! If even
I were as in my boyhood, and could be

The comrade of thy wanderings over heaven,
As then, when to outstrip thy skyey speed
Scarce seemed a vision; I would ne'er have striven

As thus with thee in prayer in my sore need.
Oh lift me as a wave, a leaf, a cloud!
I fall upon the thorns of life! I bleed!

A heavy weight of hours has chained and bowed
One too like thee – tameless, and swift, and proud.

V

Make me thy lyre, even as the forest is:
What if my leaves are falling like its own?
The tumult of thy mighty harmonies

Will take from both a deep autumnal tone,
Sweet though in sadness. Be thou, spirit fierce,
My spirit! Be thou me, impetuous one!

Drive my dead thoughts over the universe
Like withered leaves to quicken a new birth!
And, by the incantation of this verse,

Scatter, as from an unextinguished hearth
Ashes and sparks, my words among mankind!
Be through my lips to unawakened earth

The trumpet of a prophecy! Oh wind,
If winter comes, can spring be far behind?

Extract from 'On Life'

What is life? Thoughts and feelings arise, with or without our will, and we employ words to express them. We are born, and our birth is unremembered, and our infancy remembered but in fragments. We live on, and in living we lose the apprehension of life. How vain is it to think that words can penetrate the mystery of our being! Rightly used they may make evident our ignorance to ourselves, and this is much. For what are we? Whence do we come, and whither do we go? Is birth the commencement, is death the conclusion of our being? What is birth and death?

The most refined abstractions of logic conduct to a view of life which, though startling to the apprehension, is in fact that which the habitual sense of its repeated combinations has extinguished in us. It strips, as it were, the painted curtain from this scene of things. I confess that I am one of those who am unable to refuse my assent to the conclusions of those philosophers who assert that nothing exists but as it is perceived.

It is a decision against which all our persuasions struggle, and we must be long convicted before we can be convinced that the solid universe of external things is 'such stuff as dreams are made of'. The shocking absurdities of the popular philosophy of mind and matter, and its fatal consequences in morals, their violent dogmatism concerning the source of all things, had early conducted me to materialism. This materialism is a seducing system to young and superficial minds; it allows its disciples to talk, and dispenses them from thinking. But I was discontented with such a view of things as it afforded; man is a being of high aspirations 'looking both before and after', whose 'thoughts wander through eternity', disclaiming alliance with transience and decay, incapable of imagining to himself annihilation, existing but in the future and the past, being not what he is, but what he has been and shall be. Whatever may be his true and final destination, there is a spirit within him at enmity with nothingness and dissolution. This is the character of all life and being. Each is at once the centre and the circumference, the point to which all things are referred, and the line in which all things are contained.

Such contemplations as these, materialism and the popular philosophy of mind and matter alike forbid; they are only consistent with the intellectual system.

John Clare

'I Am' (1846; edited from MS)

Clare is celebrated often as a truly rural poet – a son of the soil unlike other Romantics, who could be seen as mere visitors to the countryside. And yet in his verse there is a remarkable sophistication of speculative, existential thought.

I Am

1

I am – yet what I am, none cares or knows;
   My friends forsake me like a memory lost: –
I am the self-consumer of my woes; –
   They rise and vanish in oblivion's host,
Like shadows in love's frenzied stifled throes: –
And yet I am, and live – like vapours tost

2

Into the nothingness of scorn and noise, –
   Into the living sea of waking dreams,
Where there is neither sense of life or joys,
   But the vast shipwreck of my lifes esteems;
Even the dearest, that I love the best
Are strange – nay, rather stranger than the rest.

3

I long for scenes where man hath never trod
   A place where woman never smiled or wept
There to abide with my Creator, God;
   And sleep as I in childhood, sweetly slept,
Untroubling, and untroubled where I lie,
The grass below – above the vaulted sky.

John Keats

'Ode on Melancholy' (1819) and 'Ode to a Nightingale' (1819)

Keats' work is the poetry of sensuality, and this is vividly exemplified in both of these odes (from *Lamia, Isabella, The Eve of St Agnes and Other Poems*, 1820), bringing into full play all the senses in an overpowering concoction of Romantic evocation. He is also a master poetic craftsman, hugely influential in this respect despite his untimely death.

Ode on Melancholy

1

No, no, go not to Lethe, neither twist
   Wolfsbane, tight-rooted, for its poisonous wine;
Nor suffer thy pale forehead to be kissed
   By nightshade, ruby grape of Proserpine;
Make not your rosary of yew-berries,
    Nor let the beetle, nor the death-moth be
      Your mournful Psyche, nor the downy owl
A partner in your sorrow's mysteries;
    For shade to shade will come too drowsily,
      And drown the wakeful anguish of the soul.

2

But when the melancholy fit shall fall
   Sudden from heaven like a weeping cloud,
That fosters the droop-headed flowers all,
   And hides the green hill in an April shroud;
Then glut thy sorrow on a morning rose,
   Or on the rainbow of the salt sand-wave,
    Or on the wealth of globed peonies;
Or if thy mistress some rich anger shows,
   Imprison her soft hand, and let her rave,
    And feed deep, deep upon her peerless eyes.

3

She dwells with Beauty – Beauty that must die;
   And Joy, whose hand is ever at his lips
Bidding adieu; and aching Pleasure nigh,
   Turning to poison while the bee-mouth sips.
Aye, in the very temple of Delight
   Veiled Melancholy has her sovran shrine,
    Though seen of none save him whose strenuous tongue

Can burst Joy's grape against his palate fine;
   His soul shall taste the sadness of her might,
   And be among her cloudy trophies hung.

Ode to a Nightingale

1

My heart aches, and a drowsy numbness pains
   My sense, as though of hemlock I had drunk,
Or emptied some dull opiate to the drains
   One minute past, and Lethe-wards had sunk;
'Tis not through envy of thy happy lot,
   But being too happy in thine happiness,
      That thou, light-winged dryad of the trees,
         In some melodious plot
Of beechen green, and shadows numberless,
   Singest of summer in full-throated ease.

2

Oh for a draught of vintage! that hath been
   Cooled a long age in the deep-delved earth,
Tasting of flora and the country green,
   Dance, and Provençal song, and sunburnt mirth!
Oh for a beaker full of the warm south,
   Full of the true, the blushful Hippocrene,
      With beaded bubbles winking at the brim,
         And purple-stained mouth;
That I might drink, and leave the world unseen,
   And with thee fade away into the forest dim –

3

Fade far away, dissolve, and quite forget
   What thou among the leaves hast never known,
The weariness, the fever, and the fret
   Here, where men sit and hear each other groan;
Where palsy shakes a few, sad, last grey hairs,
   Where youth grows pale, and spectre-thin, and dies;
      Where but to think is to be full of sorrow
         And leaden-eyed despairs;
Where Beauty cannot keep her lustrous eyes,
   Or new Love pine at them beyond tomorrow.

4

Away! Away! For I will fly to thee,
  Not charioted by Bacchus and his pards,
But on the viewless wings of Poesy,
  Though the dull brain perplexes and retards;
Already with thee! Tender is the night,
  And haply the Queen Moon is on her throne,
    Clustered around by all her starry fays;
      But here there is no light
Save what from heaven is with the breezes blown
  Through verdurous glooms and winding mossy ways.

5

I cannot see what flowers are at my feet,
  Nor what soft incense hangs upon the boughs,
But, in embalmed darkness, guess each sweet
  Wherewith the seasonable month endows
The grass, the thicket, and the fruit-tree wild,
  White hawthorn, and the pastoral eglantine,
    Fast-fading violets covered up in leaves,
      And mid-May's eldest child,
The coming musk-rose, full of dewy wine,
  The murmurous haunt of flies on summer eves.

6

Darkling I listen; and for many a time
  I have been half in love with easeful Death,
Called him soft names in many a mused rhyme,
  To take into the air my quiet breath;
Now more than ever seems it rich to die,
  To cease upon the midnight with no pain,
    While thou art pouring forth thy soul abroad
      In such an ecstasy!
Still wouldst thou sing, and I have ears in vain –
  To thy high requiem become a sod.

7

Thou wast not born for death, immortal bird!
  No hungry generations tread thee down;
The voice I hear this passing night was heard
  In ancient days by emperor and clown:
Perhaps the self-same song that found a path
  Through the sad heart of Ruth, when, sick for home,

She stood in tears amid the alien corn;
  The same that oft-times hath
Charmed magic casements, opening on the foam
  Of perilous seas, in fairy lands forlorn.

8

Forlorn! The very word is like a bell
  To toll me back from thee to my sole self!
Adieu! The fancy cannot cheat so well
  As she is famed to do, deceiving elf.
Adieu! Adieu! Thy plaintive anthem fades
  Past the near meadows, over the still stream,
    Up the hillside, and now 'tis buried deep
      In the next valley-glades:
Was it a vision, or a waking dream?
  Fled is that music – do I wake or sleep?

Mary Shelley

From *Frankenstein* (1818)

The awe-inspiring Alpine setting (seen through the eyes of Frankenstein himself) is all-important here, preparing the reader for the equally dramatic meeting between Frankenstein and the Creature he has created and then forsaken. The meeting takes place immediately after this extract from Chapter 10 of the novel.

I spent the following day roaming through the valley. I stood beside the sources of the Arveiron, which take their rise in a glacier, that with slow pace is advancing down from the summit of the hills, to barricade the valley. The abrupt sides of vast mountains were before me; the icy wall of the glacier overhung me; a few shattered pines were scattered around; and the solemn silence of this glorious presence-chamber of imperial Nature was broken only by the brawling waves, or the fall of some vast fragment, the thunder sound of the avalanche, or the cracking, reverberated along the mountains, of the accumulated ice, which, through the silent working of immutable laws, was ever and anon rent and torn, as if it had been but a plaything in their hands. These sublime and magnificent scenes afforded me the greatest consolation that I was capable of receiving. They elevated me from all littleness of feeling; and although they did not remove my grief, they subdued and tranquillised it. In some degree, also, they diverted my mind from the thoughts over which it had brooded for the last month. I retired to rest at night; my slumbers, as it were, waited on and ministered to by the assemblance of grand shapes which I had contemplated during the day. They congregated round me; the unstained snowy mountain-top, the glittering pinnacle, the pine woods, and ragged bare ravine; the eagle, soaring amidst the clouds – they all gathered round me, and bade me be at peace.

Where had they fled when the next morning I awoke? All of soul-inspiriting fled with sleep, and dark melancholy clouded every thought. The rain was pouring in torrents, and thick mists hid the summits of the mountains, so that I even saw not the faces of those mighty friends. Still I would penetrate their misty veil, and seek them in their cloudy retreats. What were rain and storm to me? My mule was brought to the door, and I resolved to ascend to the summit of Montanvert. I remembered the effect that the view of the tremendous and ever-moving glacier had produced upon my mind when I first saw it. It had then filled me with a sublime ecstasy that gave wings to the soul, and allowed it to soar from the obscure world to light and joy. The sight of the awful and majestic in nature had indeed always the effect of solemnising my mind, and causing me to forget the passing cares of life. I determined to go without a guide, for I was well acquainted with the path, and the presence of another would destroy the solitary grandeur of the scene.

The ascent is precipitous, but the path is cut into continual and short windings, which enable you to surmount the perpendicularity of the mountain. It is a scene terrifically desolate. In a thousand spots the traces of the winter avalanche may be perceived, where trees lie broken and strewed on the ground; some entirely destroyed, others bent, leaning upon the jutting rocks of the mountain, or transversely upon other trees. The path, as you ascend higher, is intersected by ravines of snow, down which stones continually roll from above; one of them is particularly dangerous, as the slightest sound, such as even speaking in a loud voice, produces a concussion of air sufficient to draw destruction upon the head of the speaker. The pines are not tall or luxuriant, but they are sombre, and add an air of severity to the scene. I looked on the valley beneath; vast mists were rising from the rivers which ran through it, and curling in thick wreaths around the opposite mountains, whose summits were hid in the uniform clouds, while rain poured from the dark sky, and added to the melancholy impression I received from the objects around me. Alas! why does man boast of sensibilities superior to those apparent in the brute; it only renders them more necessary beings. If our impulses were confined to hunger, thirst, and desire, we might be nearly free; but now we are moved by every wind that blows, and a chance word or scene that that word may convey to us.

'We rest; a dream has power to poison sleep.
We rise; one wand'ring thought pollutes the day.
We feel, conceive, or reason; laugh or weep,
Embrace fond woe, or cast our cares away;
It is the same: for, be it joy or sorrow,
The path of its departure still is free.
Man's yesterday may ne'er be like his morrow;
Nought may endure but mutability!'

It was nearly noon when I arrived at the top of the ascent. For some time I sat upon the rock that overlooks the sea of ice. A mist covered both that and the surrounding mountains. Presently a breeze dissipated the cloud, and I descended upon the glacier. The surface is very uneven, rising like the waves of a troubled sea, descending low, and interspersed by rifts that sink deep. The field of ice is almost a league in width, but I spent nearly two hours in crossing it. The opposite mountain is a bare perpendicular rock. From the side where I now stood Montanvert was exactly opposite, at the distance of a league; and above it rose Mont Blanc, in awful majesty. I remained in a recess of the rock, gazing on this wonderful and stupendous scene. The sea, or rather the vast river of ice, wound among its dependent mountains, whose aerial summits hung over its recesses. Their icy and glittering peaks shone in the sunlight over the clouds. My heart, which was before sorrowful, now swelled with something like joy; I exclaimed – 'Wandering spirits, if indeed ye wander, and do not rest in your narrow beds, allow me this faint happiness, or take me, as your companion, away from the joys of life.'

Elizabeth Barrett Browning

'Stanzas on the Death of Lord Byron' (1824)

Browning was 18 at the time she wrote this poem, and it certainly testifies to the attractive power of the Byron myth to the Romantic imagination. Evident too is impressive sureness of touch in handling the obvious emotional impact of her hero's death.

Stanzas on the Death of Lord Byron

He *was*, and *is* not! Graecia's trembling shore,
    Sighing through all her palmy groves, shall tell
That Harold's pilgrimage at last is o'er;
    Mute the impassioned tongue, and tuneful shell,

That erst was wont in noblest strains to swell!
Hushed the proud shouts that rode th' Aegean wave,
    For lo! the great deliv'rer breathes farewell!
Gives to the world his mem'ry, and a grave –
And dies amidst the land he lived and fought to save!

Mourn, Hellas, mourn! and o'er thy widowed brow,
    For aye the cypress wreath of sorrow twine;
And in thy new-formed beauty, desolate, throw
    The fresh-culled flowers on *his* sepulchral shrine.
    Yes, let that heart, whose fervour was all thine,
In consecrated urn lamented be!
    That generous heart whose genius thrilled divine
Hath spent its last most glorious throb for thee –
Then sank amidst the storm that made thy children free.

Britannia's poet, Graecia's hero, sleeps!
    And Freedom, bending o'er the breathless clay,
Lifts up her voice, and in her wildness weeps!
    For *us*, a night hath clouded o'er our day
    And hushed the lips that breathed our fairest lay.
Alas! and must the British lyre resound
    A requiem, while the spirit wings away
Of *him* who on her strings such music found,
And taught her startling chords to breathe so sweet a sound?

The theme grows sadder – and my soul shall find
    A language in these tears. No more, no more!
Soon, midst the shrieking of the tossing wind,
    The 'dark blue depths' he sang of shall have bore
    Our *all* of Byron to his native shore!
His grave is thick with voices, murm'ring here
    The awful tale of greatness swiftly o'er;
But mem'ry strives with death and, ling'ring near,
Shall consecrate the dust of Harold's lonely bier!

4 | Critical approaches

- How may the views of literary critics help the reader increase his or her understanding of Romantic literature?

- What should be the principal purpose of literary criticism, especially as it relates to Romanticism?

- What do the main schools of literary criticism – the psychoanalytical, Marxist, and feminist approaches, for example – have to say about Romanticism?

The nature of literary criticism

The thrust of this book has been an attempt to enable the reader to come to terms with Romanticism in context, deciding for himself or herself what views to take and judgements to make. In this process, the reasoned opinions of others, whether professional critics, teachers or fellow students, can be of immense value. There have been many quotations throughout this book from a diverse range of writers about Romanticism. These opinions and others, however, are no substitute for developing one's own literary judgement, and the critical approaches encountered in this section should be seen in this positive context.

The poet and critic W.H. Auden (1907–1973) saw a great deal of value in the processes of literary criticism, as described in his 'Reading' in *The Dyer's Hand and Other Essays* (1963). He hoped that literary critics would:

> 1 introduce me to authors or works of which I was hitherto unaware
> 2 convince me that I have undervalued an author or a work because I had not read them carefully enough
> 3 show me relations between works of different ages and cultures which I could never have seen for myself because I do not know enough and never shall
> 4 give a 'reading' of a work which increases my understanding of it
> 5 throw light upon the process of artistic 'Making'
> 6 throw light upon the relation of art to life, to science, economics, ethics, religion, etc.

These points provide an excellent foundation for considering various critical approaches to Romanticism.

In order to illustrate some of the various possible critical positions, and to give a fuller flavour of their implications, the focus in this section will be on appraisal of two key Romantic texts: the works of William Blake, and the novel *Frankenstein* by Mary Shelley. (Extracts from both have been included in Part 3: Texts and extracts.) The principal critical viewpoints which are explored here in relation to Blake and Shelley are the psychoanalytical, the Marxist and the feminist schools.

Freud and his influence

Sigmund Freud (1856–1939) is famous as the founder of psychoanalysis, and it is hard to over-estimate his importance as one of the key thinkers of the modern age. Although Freud always saw himself as a scientist, intent on providing a scientific, provable basis for his insights into the human psyche, he appreciated the huge potential significance of the arts as a key to psychology. He had a particular liking for art himself – a print of the Romantic artist Fuseli's painting 'The Nightmare' enjoyed a prominent place in his study – and saw the value of art and literature in delving into the recesses of the mind.

Since Freud's own time there have been many interpretations and developments of his work, and these have given rise to diverse insights into psychology – particularly relevant in the context of literary criticism. Often there have been – and still are – fierce conflicts between those adhering to particular strands of Freudian thought and practice, not least in the field of literary criticism. However, there are certain Freudian principles shared by all his followers: chief among them a belief that the human psyche is largely hidden from the conscious mind for most of our waking lives. According to the Freudian outlook, the conscious – often rational – part of the mind may be compared with the tip of an iceberg; underneath lurks a far larger psychic entity which Freud termed the 'subconscious'. Although largely hidden, the subconscious may be seen as the chief influence on emotions and behaviour, revealing itself vividly in dreams and in states of emotional intensity. The particular relevance of the arts here is clear, especially, perhaps, arts in the Romantic context, seeking deliberately to investigate and present the totality of human experience. Further aspects of Freudian thought which may shed light on Romanticism include:

- the focus on childhood experience as the basis of psychological development

- the particular emphasis on the relationship between parents and children, developed through the Oedipus complex

- the theory that sexuality, repressed or otherwise, lies at the root of human behaviour

- ideas centring on the psychologically divided self, especially when the 'id' (the appetite-driven emotional basis of life) is in conflict with the 'ego' (the conscious sense of 'self') or the 'super-ego' (the sense of morality, sometimes construed as the conscience)

- the death-wish as a powerful psychological drive, running counter to the desire to live and survive (Freud's 'pleasure principle'), and based on the continuing attraction of a return to the darkness and security of the womb.

Freud did not really pursue the cultural or literary-critical implications of his work, but, since his ideas became widely known, many cultural and literary commentators have applied them to their particular fields. Outside these academic disciplines several of Freud's perceptions have found their way into popular consciousness. Most people, for example, have some sense that there is such a thing as the subconscious mind, regard dreams as open to interpretation, and may use expressions like 'a Freudian slip' to denote the intrusion of the subconscious into everyday behaviour. This very ubiquity of popular Freudianism, however, may make a more subtle appreciation of his insights difficult to achieve, and care needs to be taken here to avoid 'crude' applications.

With regard to Blake's poetry, a psychoanalytical exploration would be likely to focus on the experiences and relationships of childhood and its relationship to the world: the juxtaposition of innocence and experience, in effect. Sexual imagery abounds in *Songs of Innocence and of Experience*, particularly if Blake's integral illustrations are taken into account as well. The poems frequently feature anxious boys and girls lost and found, or carefree children giving full vent to their unbridled energy before the world of experience steps in to curtail such freedom. The idea of infantile sexuality comes across strongly from many of these poems, anticipating the scientific studies made by Freud in this field by over a century. Blake's own aphorism, 'Energy is eternal delight', is appropriate here, signifying his celebration and defence of the physical and sensual sides of the human personality. He was also keenly aware of the potentially damaging effects of repression of this energy, both in childhood and – even more disastrously, given time to fester – in adulthood. Thus, in the aptly titled *Marriage of Heaven and Hell* (Heaven denoting the rational intellect, Hell the instinctive and sensual), Blake wrote:

> Those who restrain desire, do so because theirs is weak enough to be restrained; and the restrainer or reason usurps its place and governs the unwilling. And being restrained, it by degrees becomes passive, till it is only the shadow of desire.

Blake's work may be plausibly read as an exploration of this perception, from the early *Songs of Innocence* to the later densely symbolic prophetic books.

Turning to *Frankenstein*, it is possible to see the appropriateness of Freudian approaches in a number of ways. Psychological interpretations of this novel have tended to focus on notions of the subconscious, or, at a still deeper level, the unconscious. (Ideas on the possibility of a 'collective unconscious', a deep stratum of psychological reality shared by all people, were developed by the one-time follower of Freud, Carl Gustav Jung [1875–1961], with a distinctive focus on human creativity.) Frankenstein himself may be seen as representing the conscious, rational mind (he was, after all, a scientist, if a rather unconventional one), desperately trying to impose his egotistical will on the forces of nature. Interestingly, the idea of the ego as embodying the will of the conscious mind over the rampant emotions of the 'id' is centrally Freudian – as is the sense that this attempt is doomed to failure unless the power of the 'id' is fully acknowledged. In the novel, Frankenstein certainly discovered this, if the Creature is seen as symbolising the release of uncontrolled dark forces somehow created by the human psyche yet chillingly apart from it. The extract from *Frankenstein,* included on page 103, illustrates the typically Romantic Alpine setting for the eventual meeting between creator and Creature, emphasising their essential unity and their powerlessness in the face of dramatic nature – another favourite Romantic notion.

Significantly, in view of the long discussions on the role of the artist that Mary Shelley had with her husband and other centrally Romantic figures like Byron, the novel tells us much about the idea of the Romantic artist. Whereas Frankenstein is led inexorably to his own destruction through his failure to come to terms with his darker side – the Creature – the essence of the truly Romantic artist was precisely to acknowledge, and creatively use, all aspects of the human psyche. The close links between Freudian psychology and the beliefs of the Romantics are apparent here, and it may well be – despite Freud's insistence on the scientific validity of his ideas – that the roots of psychoanalysis itself are to be found in Romanticism.

▶ Consider the elements of Freudian thought as outlined above and discuss whether and how they could help your understanding of other Romantic texts you have read. If so, how helpful do you think Freudian approaches are in developing a critical appreciation of Romanticism generally?

▶ In this context, reflect on the presentation of sexuality and parent-child relationships in poems by Blake. To what extent does a Freudian analysis help to explain the complex sexuality of infants featured in *Songs of Innocence and of Experience*?

Marx and his influence

Marxist approaches to literature contrast with those of Freud and his followers in emphasising the social context and implications of texts, rather than psychological investigations of authors and their fictional creations. There need not necessarily be a contradiction between the two approaches, although they are very different philosophically. Basically, the Freudian, psychoanalytical position holds that the individual's psychology largely determines his or her social interaction, whereas for the Marxist it is the social context – the material, objective reality, as Marxists are fond of saying – which in the end determines any one individual's psychology.

Different emphases have developed within the broad school of Marxist criticism. Historical approaches attempt to ground texts and their authors firmly in their social and political contexts and have generally arrived at a reading of those texts through a study of history. Marxist critics of this kind tend to see cultural expressions, including literature, as manifestations of historical struggles and values. Other critics working within the broad field of Marxism tend towards more distinctively literary approaches, often focusing on the social struggles documented within the texts themselves. This documentation may be the author's conscious intention, but often it was not – this makes little difference to the critic. Implied here is rather greater significance for literature itself: art may have a powerful impact on social and political forces, as well as initially reflecting them.

Wherever the emphasis, Marxist criticism has tended to distance itself from what may be seen as the crude materialism of its early days, whereby the arts were seen merely as a passive reflection of far greater historical and economic forces. The philosophical tool used to achieve greater subtlety in analysing the relationship between texts and social contexts is the dialectical method. Through this method it is possible to see any historical phenomenon, including literature, in terms of a struggle between a thesis and its antithesis. The conflict between the two leads to a new stage of reality, a synthesis. This in turn becomes part of a new struggle with its own opposite (antithesis) in a fresh process of transformation. Thus history is never static. In terms of application to Romanticism, the writer or artist inevitably reflects part of the original struggle within society, but the work of art itself could be seen as a new synthesis. In its turn, this synthesis will become part of a new conflict. It is clear that the role of the artist is, potentially at least, an important one.

The social and political contexts of Romantic literature have been emphasised throughout this book. It is no accident that Marxism as a school of thought emerged during the period of Romanticism, broadly, as the fast-emerging capitalism of the late 18th and early 19th centuries made for unsettled, often embattled times. Marxism itself, despite the fact that Marx, like Freud, saw himself as a scientist, may be seen as an essentially Romantic phenomenon. In this respect, art played an important part in the understanding and appreciation of history. A later Marxist, Leon Trotsky (1879–1940), who, as commander of the Red Army during the Russian Revolution of 1917, certainly knew embattled times, stressed the particular significance and special appeal of literature. In his polemical essay 'Class and Art' (1924), Trotsky wrote of the continuing appeal of Dante's *Divine Comedy*, though his words could really apply to important art of any period:

> Works of art developed in a medieval Italian city can, we find, affect us too. What does this require? A small thing: it requires that these feelings and moods shall have received such broad, intense, powerful expression as to have raised them above the limitations of the life of those days.

Above all, for the Marxist, literature connects dynamically and in complex ways with its social, political and economic contexts.

Marxist contributions to literary criticism include:

- an interest in the means by which texts are produced and distributed, and how these may influence the nature of those texts

- discovering the ways in which a text was read by contemporaries in terms of its perceived social or political 'message' or imagery

- exploration of the particular historical point at which the text emerged, with emphasis on the social and economic conflicts of the time

- an analysis of how plot, characters and setting may reflect these conflicts through what is included in the text, or, interestingly, what is left out

- a particular interest in how characters may become 'outsider' figures, feeling alienated from their social context – their fellow human beings.

▶ In the light of your reading of Romantic texts and about their social context, consider how some of the approaches listed above may apply. Do they in any way aid understanding of the texts?

▶ How might Marxist interpretive models relate to those used by Freudian, psychological criticism? As a focus here, develop any insights already gained into key texts to include references to class relationships.

The Marxist position on Blake would, for example, emphasise his revolutionary credentials in the context of the social upheavals of his world. This point of view has been convincingly stated by the critic Edward Larrisey in his *William Blake* (1985). He follows Terry Eagleton's sense of Blake as 'England's greatest revolutionary artist' in his analysis of Blake's critique of the uses and abuses of power:

> Many of Blake's poems are criticisms of oppressive uses of power on many levels, and they imply that there is a link between the use of power when one individual belittles another and the use of power on a large political and economic scale.

Thus the various relationships portrayed in *Songs of Innocence and of Experience*, which when read from a psychoanalytical point of view suggest issues focusing on the personal psyche and its immediate problems, for the Marxist embody class and power orientated relationships. Taking this interpretive position with regard to one of the most famous of the *Songs*, 'The Tiger', for instance, it may be that the tiger itself is a symbol of political oppression irreconcilable with the placid goodness of the lamb in the *Innocence* poem of that name. The tiger, the natural oppressor of the lamb, is apparently all-powerful, but in reality – and this would certainly be borne out by the toy-like, harmless appearance of Blake's illustration of the tiger – is nothing but a sham: a paper tiger, in effect, deserving of a swift overthrow, very much like the precarious ruling class in Blake's Britain.

Using Marxist approaches: *Frankenstein*

Marxist criticism would be likely to place the text and its production firmly in its time – in effect this means an exploration of the social and economic conditions. The early 19th century was a period of dramatic expansion of capitalism as the dominant economic system for Western Europe, with the accompanying growth of both middle and working classes – the former finding wealth in employing (or exploiting, as Marxists would say) the latter, to over-simplify somewhat. The resulting class conflict may be reflected in the novel *Frankenstein*, written by a young female author of radical parentage (Godwin and Wollstonecraft) and newly married to a revolutionary poet, Shelley, who spent much of his considerable heritage on trying to finance rebellion in Ireland. The novel can be read as either a revolutionary or reactionary text, and in that sense mirrors a certain ambivalence in Mary Shelley's own character – she was at once sympathetic to the radical cause and fearful of the violent consequences of revolution. Indeed, in her travels through Europe with Shelley, she witnessed some of the chaotic and destructive aftermath of revolution and war. In later life, Mary Shelley wrote that the radicals 'are full of repulsion to me – violent without any sense of Justice'. In this political and social ambivalence she typified the radical intellectuals of the period, and her work is all the more fascinating for this.

To follow through the implications of such an analysis for the reading of *Frankenstein* with a Marxist perspective is potentially illuminating. The reading may well focus on ambivalence, both from characters within the text and from the reader's viewpoint, towards the Creature. Marxist critics have drawn attention to the historical similarities between the language popularly used at the time to describe the growing working class – the Marxists' proletariat – and the language used by Mary Shelley to evoke her Creature. If in some sense the Creature can be seen as emblematic of the proletariat in terms of its power and in the limits of this power, the novel as a whole makes sense. Further, the proletariat owes its very existence, miserable as it may be, to the exploitative needs of the respectable middle class – the Marxists' 'bourgeoisie' – as personified by the academic Frankenstein, who above all seeks to control nature. But in the novel the Creature frees himself, even beginning to dictate terms to his creator. Ultimately creator and Creature are alienated from each other, as, in the Marxist scheme of things, the capitalist and working classes will inevitably be alienated from each other through the processes of history. By the end of the novel, neither has the ascendancy – each in fact virtually ensures the other's destruction, despite their closeness – but a Marxist reading may well locate this failure to resolve the novel's conflict in the failure of Mary Shelley, and her class, to acknowledge the inevitable victory of the proletariat.

Feminist approaches

Freudian and Marxist literary approaches have played crucial roles in the development of feminist criticism, as have the insights gained through structuralist and post-structuralist criticism, particularly those focusing on the relationships between texts and readers, and on the 'silences' of texts. The growth of feminism as a social movement in the 20th century demanded a reappraisal of literature. Basically, there have been two strands involved, often inter-related. On the one hand, critics have concentrated on re-evaluating and re-interpreting literature already in the academic domain (and written, for the most part, by men). On the other hand, there have been moves towards establishing and developing a particularly female tradition in literature through the discovery and promotion of 'lost' or comparatively neglected women writers.

In fact, feminist approaches to literature began in the Romantic age through the agency of key Romantic figures: with the writings of Mary Wollstonecraft, Mary Shelley's mother, and those who followed her. Men too began to re-appraise the literary portrayal of women. Coleridge, for example, made the essentially feminist point that Matthew Lewis (1775–1818), in his gothic novel *The Monk*, reduced female characters to either 'trembling innocence' or 'shameless harlotry' and then went on to exploit both male-orientated models of femininity as, in Coleridge's words, 'vehicles of the most voluptuous images'.

Blake in many ways is a problematic figure in feminist terms: energetically radical in both personal and social spheres, he nevertheless maintained a symbolic language in which the female is distinctly more passive than the male. He could be refreshingly direct in his approach to sexuality, couching his views in a way to emphasise sexual equality, as in his verse fragment 'The Question Answered':

What is it men in women do require?
The lineaments of gratified desire.
What is it women in men do require?
The lineaments of gratified desire.

At work here, almost certainly, is the radical feminist influence of Mary Wollstonecraft, whom Blake knew and deeply respected. However, Peter Ackroyd, in his biography *Blake* (1995), has suggested that

> ... in his poetry there are ... images of fear and revulsion; the horror of the female (together with the horror of passivity and softness) is forcefully expressed, while the dread of female power and female domination becomes a constant refrain.

Such a view certainly appears damning enough. One way of coming to terms with this apparently reactionary position, however, might be to suggest that Blake was concerned ultimately with male and female as symbolic entities in his analysis: facets of the human psyche whether male or female in effect, rather than men and women as such. If this angle is taken, Blake's insistence that the whole range of psychic forces be brought into play – what in modern parlance might be called the masculine and feminine 'sides' – could be seen as powerfully, liberatingly feminist. Such a view would also connect with the analytical psychologist Jung, one time collaborator with Freud before both went separate personal and theoretical ways. Jung coined the terms 'anima' and 'animus' for the female aspect of the male psyche and the male aspect of the female psyche respectively, developing theories to explore the damaging effects of the repression of either.

In such areas of feminist concern as the relative silence or passivity of female literary characters, the hostility of reviewers to female authors, and patronising (if often well-meant) revisions of women's writing by men along 'conventional' lines, *Frankenstein* again provides a key example. Much feminist criticism has focused on the novel as an exploration and exposure of the folly of male posturing – the narrowly ambitious scientist intent on the domination of nature. In this, the character of Frankenstein reflected contemporary scientific discourse, at once adventurously pioneering and dangerously limited in ethical concern. Humphrey Davy, for example, an eminent scientist read and admired by both Shelleys, enthused about science enabling 'man' to

> ... change and modify the beings surrounding him, and by his experiments to interrogate nature with power, not simply as a scholar, passive and seeking only to understand her operations, but rather as a master, active with his own instruments.
>
> (from *A Discourse, introductory to a Course of Lectures on Chemistry*, 1802)

Striking here is the concept of mastery, and the male principle is conventionally emphasised by the use of gendered pronouns. Romanticism, in an important sense, attempted to re-establish a connection between intellect and feeling – and in this, it has a direct relevance to the feminist critique of the male-orientated social and literary worlds. *Frankenstein* may justifiably be read in this light, as illustrating the disastrous consequences of the separation of the two human characteristics.

The location of power is crucial here, both for this text and for feminist criticism generally. Even before Frankenstein begins his story, the 'framing' narrator Walton writes of his quest for 'the dominion I should acquire and transmit over the elemental foes of our race', thus establishing the tone for Frankenstein's own ambitions. Mary Shelley subtly undermines and questions such male assumptions throughout the novel, using the text as a prophecy in the sense that William Blake meant when he wrote of a true prophet not foretelling a pre-determined future, but rather warning: 'Thus: if you go on So, the result is So.' (from *Marginalia*, 1798). Frankenstein not only seeks to impose his will on nature, he actually usurps woman's maternal role in his plan to create human life itself. In this he is ultimately thwarted, resulting in a disastrous distortion of female biological creativity.

Furthermore, the women in the novel are unwilling and powerless, in this competitively masculine world, to stop him. In effect, they speak with subdued voices, or are virtually silent. Frankenstein's mother scarcely appears at all. His fiancée Elizabeth is passive and undemanding, seen almost entirely through the eyes of Frankenstein in what verges on an incestuous relationship. His adoptive sister Justine is an even more shadowy figure: an habitual victim eventually sacrificed to the avenging Creature. Agatha is largely silent, lacking any vitality, and Safie's fairy-tale feminine sweetness is almost entirely focused on her lover Felix. Significantly, Frankenstein cannot bring himself to create a female counterpart to his male Creature, destroying at the last moment all his work towards that end.

The actual production of the novel has attracted further feminist attention. It has been noted, for example, that Mary's husband Percy Shelley revised huge sections of the writing, sometimes replacing the stylistic directness with a more 'sophisticated' tone and punctuating the prose throughout. It is possible to argue, as has Anne Mellor, that these revisions 'actually distorted the meaning of the text'. Such was the power of the (male) reviewers that when Mary Shelley published the novel, in 1818, she felt compelled to do so anonymously. In a final patronising insult, many readers and reviewers were so impressed by the book they assumed it must have been written by a man, probably her husband. In fact, Mary Shelley did not acknowledge authorship of *Frankenstein* until some years later in 1823, by which time Percy was already, ironically and tragically, dead.

▶ Consider further the points made above in relation to the novel *Frankenstein*. Do you think they could be usefully applied to other Romantic texts? If so, which ones?

Assignments

1 Having been introduced to some of the possible critical approaches to Romanticism, and seen how they may be applied to Blake and Mary Shelley, consider how appropriate these approaches may be to other examples. It may be best to focus on one short text, perhaps taken from Part 3: Texts and extracts, and then apply a particular interpretive model to this text. Aim to construct a carefully reasoned justification of your particular 'reading', and go on to present the various approaches in a structured 'critics' debate' session.

   What are the strengths and weaknesses of the different interpretations? How may some models be more apt for certain texts than others?

2 In order more fully to explore the possibilities and validity of different readings of your chosen text(s), try developing particular interpretations for one or more of a range of contexts. These could include:
   • a film director considering ideas for a short film version, adapting and selecting material as appropriate
   • a graphic artist working on illustrations of key moments in the text, to accompany a new edition for a specific audience
   • a documentary maker focusing on the biography of the writer of the text, seeking to integrate the life story with the text itself
   • a writer of an abridged version for a particular readership, working on the selection of what is deemed most significant in the text
   • an historian accumulating evidence, from texts and contexts, in order to come to a fuller understanding of the epoch involved.

3 Returning briefly to W.H. Auden's formulation of what he would expect of a good literary critic (quoted on page 107), consider carefully which – if any – of his six points have been met in your own encounters with literary criticism of Romantic texts.

   It may be especially worthwhile to discuss Auden's fourth point ('Give a 'reading' of a work which increases my understanding of it') and add the word 'enjoyment'. Has an enhanced critical sense added to your textual understanding or enjoyment?

   In the light of the six requirements, which critical approach, or synthesis of more than one, is closest to your own views?

5 | How to write about Romanticism

It is important to realise that there is no single 'best way' to write about Romanticism. In a sense, the very spirit of Romanticism itself implies diversity in interpretation and in the style of written response – anything else might be rather inappropriate or merely formulaic. Each writer has to find his or her own way in to the subject, adopting an appropriate and lively style as befits the nature of Romanticism itself. Nevertheless, there are useful guidelines and suggestions which may aid the writing process: spontaneous originality by itself would be unlikely to produce effective, well structured written responses, and any perceptive insights may well remain hidden in the confusion. This point is especially valid for the writing about Romantic literature in its various contexts, as has been illustrated in the many quotations throughout this book from commentators on Romanticism. In writing about Romantic texts, it may be helpful to ask three basic questions about the text, all of which point to an appreciation of wider contexts:

- What type of text is this? (a sense of genre)
- Who wrote the text? for whom? when? (an appreciation of purpose)
- In what ways may it be read? (insights into audience)

These questions and their implications need further examination.

A sense of genre

The type, or genre, of the text being considered has a great deal to tell us about the sort of characteristics to expect. Each genre has its own conventions and likely features. It is possible to divide texts into broad categories – novels, poems and plays, for example – and call these 'genres'. So, a novel is usually of a certain length, is organised in chapters, and tells some sort of story. A poem's features are likely to include rhythmic structure and concentrated language; those of a play might include a focus on dialogue and structural organisation into acts and scenes. However, these must be seen as very broad genres, and genre studies usually explore more subtle distinctions and relationships between and within texts. So, for instance, a Romantic poem by Coleridge may be, amongst other possibilities, a ballad, a lyric poem, or a conversational poem; in each case there are stylistic and other generic conventions to explore.

It is also clear that, in order for literature to develop and change, the forms must change: boundaries be pushed back, 'rules' broken, conventions re-invented. With reference to Romanticism, this observation seems particularly apt, as writers borrowed, developed and transcended the formal requirements of the genres to transform them. The very word 'transform' implies this sort of change. There have been several examples of this process already featured in this book: consider, for instance, Mary Shelley's use of gothic conventions in her writing of *Frankenstein*, which is fundamentally a philosophical novel. Or Coleridge taking the ballad form as the basis for his metaphysical exploration in 'The Rime of the Ancient Mariner'.

As these brief examples demonstrate, it is possible, and desirable, to refine notions of genre beyond the basic sense of whether a text is a novel, play or poem. There are within each of these genres many sub-divisions: a ballad, for example, has quite different formal characteristics from a short lyric poem, and a lengthy novel such as *Frankenstein* progresses in quite different ways from a short story. There are also generic considerations which link texts that superficially appear quite different from one another. So, in writing about genre in Romantic literature, there are several dimensions to bear in mind. It is important to be aware of genre considerations and stylistic conventions, including some of these possibilities:

- the basic distinction between broad genres such as novels, poems and plays

- refinements within these categories, such as lyric poetry or ballads, with an awareness of how the generic conventions might influence the writing

- cross-genre dimensions – either in the sense of common ground between texts apparently from different genres, or of adaptations of texts from one genre to another

- the relationship between form and content, and in particular how an author may transcend, develop or subvert a genre's conventions in order to convey his or her message.

An appreciation of purpose

A sense of purpose is vital for the effectiveness of any text; the problem is that the purpose may be difficult to discern, and in any case may differ widely depending upon who the reader actually is. Questions of authorial identity, intended audience and historical context are all relevant in this respect. With this in mind, here are three brief examples from Romantic texts.

> Oh Rose, thou art sick;
> The invisible worm
> That flies in the night
> In the howling storm

Has found out thy bed
Of crimson joy,
And his dark secret love
Does thy life destroy

(William Blake 'The Sick Rose', 1794)

A slumber did my spirit seal,
I had no human fears
She seemed a thing that could not feel
The touch of earthly years.

No motion has she now, no force;
She neither hears nor sees;
Rolled round in earth's diurnal course
With rocks and stones and trees!

(William Wordsworth 'A Slumber did my Spirit Seal', 1798)

I met a lady in the meads,
Full beautiful – a fairy's child;
Her hair was long, her foot was light,
And her eyes were wild.

(John Keats, from 'La Belle Dame Sans Merci', 1819)

These poems (the last an extract from a longer poem) were written by three of the key Romantic poets featured in this book. All three are focused on the enigmatic, elemental qualities of love, either idealised or realistic, and all use evocative natural imagery to express the powerful emotions aroused. All are written by male poets, and the subject appears to be female: this may provide a helpful clue in coming to an understanding of what is said. So there are significant similarities, but there are also, clearly, important differences. If writing comparatively about Romantic texts, the focus could be on both aspects: 'compare and contrast', as the stock literature question may instruct. In the context of an appreciation of purpose, responses to these texts could usefully centre on:

- your own reactions to the different pieces, based on a close reading

- the stylistic differences as reflecting the different poets' characteristics

- the diverse authorial intentions represented here, as discovered through research into their backgrounds

- generic similarities in terms of both style and content – perhaps introducing a consideration of just how significant historical context may be

- an emphasis on the intended readerships, and how readers' expectations may have altered over the 200 years (or perhaps remained remarkably similar) since the time of writing.

Insights into audience

Ultimately, any effective writing on Romantic texts must come to terms with a range of critical appraisals, but must also pursue its own interpretive direction. It is important to remember that, as writer, you are representing an audience, with views as valid as anyone else's – as long as they are carefully rooted in the texts and contexts. (Much useful information may be gained in this respect from Part 4, on critical approaches to Romanticism.)

However, it is as well to be aware of various critical opinions – not simply to impress your reader (this approach would be disastrous, in fact, but it remains all too common), but to refine further your own views in relation to those held by others. You could envisage your writing as a dialogue: both with particular texts, and with the opinions of various other readers. Some of these you may wish to challenge, others may be more agreeable; the point is that no opinion has arrived from nowhere in some sort of critical vacuum, so connections need to be made.

Helpful guiding questions to bear in mind while exploring the use of critical appraisals and their relationship to your own reading might include:

- How precisely does the critic's reading coincide with or differ from your own interpretation?
- How may we contextualise critics' views in terms of their philosophical standpoint and the particular preoccupations arising?
- How have critical appraisals changed over time, echoing broader developments in critical and popular taste?
- How might the views of other readers be used constructively to amplify, develop, challenge or refine your argument?

Part of a writer's skill in effectively presenting a critique of literature, Romantic or otherwise, is to weave together a range of approaches, based around the essential questions: 'Who reads the text?' and 'In what ways may it be read?' Attitudes towards and opinions of key Romantic texts and their writers have featured prominently throughout this book, and such views provide a rich sense of context. But every reader, and for that matter every writer, has to discover afresh the impact of the text itself. Good critical writing conveys this sense above all else, and by so doing remains true to the spirit of Romanticism.

Assignments

1 Romanticism has been attacked as mere 'spilt religion'. With reference to at least two Romantic texts, discuss whether this indictment has any validity.

2 In what senses is it appropriate to regard Romanticism as essentially a reaction to rationalist, Classical conceptions of life and art? Refer to at least two separate texts.

3 In what ways is it appropriate to see Romanticism as a strongly emotional aesthetic force? Consider this question in relation to chosen texts and to other art forms such as painting or music.

4 How far does Romanticism remain elusive as a literary force, impossible to define or pin down? Referring to two or more texts, might this be seen as a strength or a weakness?

5 Discuss the presentation of women in any two Romantic texts, showing how different, perhaps opposing, interpretations are possible.

6 Margaret Drabble defined Romanticism as '... an extreme assertion of the self and the value of individual experience. ... The stylistic keynote ... is intensity, and its watchword is "Imagination".' Consider how far this formulation applies to any two texts.

6 | Resources

Further reading

Primary texts

Listed here are the key Romantic texts referred to throughout this book. There are, of course, many others; this is a selection, intended to give a 'taste' of Romantic literature.

William Blake *Selected Works* (ed. David Stevens, Cambridge University Press, 1995)

Samuel Taylor Coleridge *Biographia Literaria* (ed. G. Watson, Everyman, 1991)

Mary Shelley *Frankenstein*, 1818 (ed. David Stevens, Cambridge University Press, 1998)

Dorothy Wordsworth *Journals of Dorothy Wordsworth* (ed. M. Moorman, Oxford University Press, 1973)

D. Wu (ed.) *Romanticism: an Anthology* (Blackwell, 2000)
A superbly comprehensive collection of texts, including most of those referred to in this book. Selection and editing are helpful, as is the accompanying CD Rom.

Contextual and critical texts

Peter Ackroyd *Blake* (Read, 1998)
An authoritative, entertaining biography.

David Blayney Brown *Romanticism* (Phaidon, 2001)
Wide-ranging, although focused on pictorial art, with copious, helpful illustrations.

Marilyn Butler *Romantics, Rebels and Reactionaries: English Literature and its Background 1760–1830* (Oxford University Press, 1981)
Detailed, readable contextualisation.

Aidan Day *Romanticism (The New Critical Idiom* series, Routledge, 1996)
Helpfully discursive, covering a range of viewpoints on Romanticism.

Boris Ford (ed.) *The Romantic Age in Britain (Cambridge Cultural History* series,
Cambridge University Press, 1992)
Clearly presented and covering a range of artistic and cultural dimensions.

Lilian R. Furst (ed.) *European Romanticism: Self Definition* (Methuen, 1980)
As the subtitle suggests, an apt anthology of defining characteristics.

Marilyn Gaull *English Romanticism: The Human Context* (Norton, 1988)
Usefully and vividly setting the historical scene.

Richard Holmes *Coleridge: Early Visions* and *Coleridge: Darker Reflections*
(Hodder and Stoughton, 1989 and Harper Collins, 1998 respectively).
Superb biographical writing, richly illuminating.

Hugh Honour *Romanticism* (Penguin, 1991)
A helpful survey of the arts in context.

Raymond Lister *British Romantic Painting* (Cambridge University Press, 1989)
Well introduced, with beautifully reproduced illustrations.

Andrew Motion *Keats* (Faber, 1997)
A thoughtful, meticulous biography by the current Poet Laureate.

Herbert Read *Wordsworth* (Faber, 1953)
Remains a compelling account by the famous art critic.

William St Clair *The Godwins and the Shelleys* (Faber, 1989)
Fascinating group biography, giving a vividly evocative picture of the times.

David Stevens *The Gothic Tradition* (Cambridge University Press, 2000)
A companion book in the *Cambridge Contexts in Literature* series.

E.P. Thompson *Witness against the Beast: William Blake and the Moral Law*
(Cambridge University Press, 1994)
Authoritatively places Blake in the radical tradition.

William Vaughan *Romantic Art* (Thames and Hudson, 1994)
Another very useful survey of the arts, well illustrated throughout.

J.R. Watson *English Poetry of the Romantic Period 1789–1830* (Longman, 1985)
Detailed critical survey of the key poets and their work.

ICT resources

There is a vast range available, and more appear daily. Using a search engine is
probably the best way to keep up to date. Here are a few of the more useful sites:

Romanticism on the Net (a well-established broadly-based site) at
www.ron.umontreal.ca

An academic exchange of ideas on the Romantic, named Romantic Circles, at
www.rc.umd.edu

Artistic surveys, including many Romantic artists, at
www.artchive.com
www.artcyclopedia.com
www.artlex.com

Further general sites, both helpful, at
www.eup.ed.ac.uk/journals/Romanticism
www.uh.edu/engines/romanticism

Glossary of critical and historical terms

Classicism (or, more accurately, **Neo-Classicism**) may be seen as an essential accompaniment to the Enlightenment: a belief in moderation and good order in life and art, harking back to what were felt to be classical models from ancient Greece and Rome.

The Enlightenment refers to the developing interest, during the 18th century and in Western Europe particularly, in the power of rational thought to explain the nature of existence. Implied too is a belief in inexorable human progress towards perfection through reason and science, eradicating superstition and irrationality on the way.

The gothic in many respects the opposite of the Classical outlook. Characteristic of the gothic would be a taste for exotic locations, darkly passionate emotions, sinister narratives and deliberately outlandish, shocking manifestations. The gothic could be seen as an extreme form of Romanticism, especially popular during the latter half of the 18th century and the early years of the 19th.

Imagery generally, any figurative, non-literal, language – including poetic devices such as metaphors and similes – aimed at evoking pictorial images in the mind of the reader or listener. Thus, if successful, imagery appeals less to the analytical intellect, more to that favourite Romantic concept, the imagination.

Patriarchy a social order in which men, and, more broadly, all things male, are the dominant force. This dominance may be achieved and sustained through a variety of obvious (including the use or threat of force) and more subtle means, depending on other social factors at work.

The sublime a key term in the development of Romanticism. Essentially concerned with feelings of spiritual awe and wonder, often occasioned by an emotional response to natural grandeur. Mountainous landscapes, for example, were increasingly seen as appropriate settings for sublimity of feeling. Although an ancient term, it was given new life in the 18th and 19th centuries – notably in Burke's *A Philosophical Enquiry into the Origin of Our Ideas of the Sublime and Beautiful* (1757).

Symbolism in effect, the central imagery of a given work of art or poetry, in which the image is especially redolent of other possible meanings and connotations. A modern Irish painter has described the symbol as 'the bridge between the known and the unknown, the link between conscious and unconscious' – and as such its centrality to Romantic art is abundantly clear.

Index